FRENCH DAZE

FRENCH DAZE

John Lowey

The Book Guild Ltd
Sussex, England

The Book Guild Ltd,
25 High Street,
Lewes, Sussex

First published 1999
© John Lowey 1999

Set in Times
Typesetting by
SetSystems Ltd, Saffron Walden, Essex

Printed in Great Britain by
Bookcraft (Bath) Ltd, Avon

A catalogue record for this book is
available from the British Library

ISBN 1 85776 450 1

CONTENTS

1

'BEGIN AT THE BEGINNING'
Lewis Carroll: *Alice's Adventures in Wonderland*

'France,' announced my father, looking up from his armchair next to the wireless and with an expression of shocked amazement upon his face. 'France has capitulated.' A silence fell upon the family at this news, although at only nine years of age I was far too young to understand what he was talking about. My sister was so immersed in her weekly copy of *Picturegoer* and mooning over photographs of her latest Hollywood heart-throb that even if Dad had announced the imminent end of the world it is doubtful that she would have paid more than a passing attention to his words. My mother's reaction, however, which took the form of a call upon God to help us all, was enough to alarm me into thinking that on her scale of disasters both events must be of roughly equal importance. My parents looked at each other, and had Spike Milligan been amongst us at that moment he would no doubt have interjected 'What are we going to do now?'

Despite my parents' initial fears the Germans did not invade us the next day. Father, who ran a shop or two in Liverpool, did his bit of firewatching and Mother stuck paper strips all over the windows and then had a man in to reinforce the staircase, underneath which she placed a mattress, providing, so she believed, a reasonable air raid shelter for the family. A number of concrete pyramids were placed on the shore at Formby and these our local ARP warden assured us would be most effective in stopping tanks. To my childish brain it appeared unlikely that the Germans would sail up the Mersey but I supposed that they could prove of some use should

1

England ever be invaded from the Isle of Man. Meanwhile, armed with pikes, the recently recruited Home Guard drilled in the local school yard, with only grit and determination to compensate for their lack of fire-power. Defences of one sort or another prepared, it was then just a question of wait and see.

The war years brought to Liverpool not only the bombing, which reached a climax in May 1941 when the city burned away for three days, but also succeeding waves of foreign soldiers. First came the French sailors, then the American soldiers, then the Italian prisoners and finally a Johnny-come-lately in the form of Italian soldiers, all of whom in their turn were billeted on Aintree racecourse. An interested observer could have diagnosed the progress of the war by the colour of the uniforms which paraded in twos and threes along Walton Vale, making themselves popular with the local talent and unpopular with the local males.

No doubt it was the Americans who brought the greatest change to our lives and, being fortunate enough to have an attractive sister in her late teens, their arrival brought me such luxuries as spearmint chewing gum, Hershey bars and pineapple juice in khaki-coloured cans, while my father found Lucky Strike a blessed relief from the Pasha Turkish cigarettes he had been coughing on for the last couple of years. The two women of the family meanwhile seemed to be transported to a sort of nylon heaven and my sister stopped painting her legs with carrot juice. Personally I never could understand their preference for articles of clothing over the delights offered by Wrigleys, but then I didn't understand women at that time, come to think of it, I doubt that I do even now.

Despite the goodies provided by the Americans, the GIs did not fascinate me in the way I had been fascinated by the French sailors a year or so earlier. Brought up between our home in Liverpool and the family home on the Isle of Man all things to do with the sea represented adventure for me and each week I would buy *The Navy* magazine and long for the day when I would be old enough to join the Royal Navy and wear bell-bottomed trousers.

Although there were always plenty of sailors to be seen on the streets of Liverpool and although I thought they were all heroes, it was the red pompom of the French sailors and the strange language they spoke which attracted my attention. Armed with a school exercise book and a pencil, I would stop them and ask them for some sort of written souvenir for my collection. My mother, noticing my interest, took to inviting one or two of the sailors to Sunday tea from time to time and upon these occasions she would also invite her younger sister Ethel, who had actually had a holiday abroad once before the war. My mother laboured under the mistaken belief that two weeks in Switzerland had given her sister a command of Continental languages and a way with foreigners. In fact no one in the family knew one word of French outside of the few words visible on an HP sauce bottle, and none of the French sailors we invited spoke a word of English. Despite this difficulty, most of them, by the use of many gestures and facial expressions, managed to convey the message that they believed that they had been betrayed by their government and that they did not accept they had lost the war. Problematic though any communication was, the sailors seemed pleased to be at home with us and even to relish their Sunday tea, which in wartime Liverpool is saying something.

Therefore at the impressionable age of nine my first contact with foreigners had been with the French, and although by the end of the war I had met with many Americans and even one or two Italians, it was the French that fascinated me the most. I made up my mind that one day when the war was over and I was grown up I would visit their country.

'Days of wine and roses'
Ernest Dowson: *Vitae Summa Brevis*

It was with an uncomprehending and somewhat suspicious eye that I regarded the bidet in the bedroom of the small *auberge* some 100 miles south of Calais, where I had chosen to spend my first night on French soil. *La patronne*, a little woman of

3

indeterminate but apparently considerable age, had taken great pains to inform me both loudly and in slowly delivered French monosyllables, a communication that she further enhanced by graphic and to me unsettling gestures, that its purpose was for washing specific parts of my body and not for relieving myself. It was as well that she had told me this for I had never seen a bidet before and I had been puzzling over its purpose ever since I had clapped my eyes upon the thing. Bidets were not in vogue in our part of Liverpool. My mother's sensibilities would have been shocked that plumbing even existed for such a purpose and had she reflected upon the matter she would, no doubt, have concluded that only the French could have conceived of such a device.

However, such musings did nothing to answer my urgent need to relieve an overfull bladder and the lavatory arrangements provided by the *auberge* proved difficult to locate. When at last I did find them, guided more by my olfactory sense than by any directions given by *La patronne* – she had only pointed vaguely towards a collection of ruined outhouses – they were such that I rather wished I hadn't. I was even tempted to return to the bidet, considering that it offered a far more attractive alternative in satisfying my immediate need. However, English discipline, combined with a fear that *La patronne* would certainly have some mysterious way of knowing, restrained me from using it. It would have to be the hole in the ground. Leaving the toilet area as quickly as nature permitted, and relieved in more ways than one, I returned to the *auberge*, where further investigation seemed to indicate that the bidet offered the only source of running water available to the guest. Such was my introduction to French plumbing and as a consequence of this discovery I went to bed unwashed.

The following morning, still unwashed, I tasted my first Continental breakfast of warm croissants washed down with a bowl of black coffee, after which I bid a fond farewell to Madame. Then the motorcycle and I headed southwards towards Paris. The road was empty and neither the bike nor I was familiar with the roads of France. We had served our

4

apprenticeships on twisting, rolling English roads and were delighted to discover long straights stretching into the far distance without a bend in sight. I crouched low behind the handlebars with my body horizontal to the petrol tank in true Manx TT fashion, and at full throttle we roared through the lingering early morning mists of Picardy. With a youthful confidence based upon having the right of way, and reinforced by the apparent lack of any other vehicle on the road, I ignored the occasional piratical skull and crossbones road signs that indicated a crossroads. Thankfully the guardian angel who sometimes takes care of young idiots must have been hovering in our vicinity that day and we were not reduced to a mangled heap of blood and twisted metal by collision with an ambling farm cart or any other slow-moving vehicle. An hour or so later, as we approached the capital, a marked increase in traffic demanded more caution. However, even at a reduced speed I still expected to be in Paris for lunch.

It was my first visit to France, in fact my first experience outside the United Kingdom. At home the Attlee government was in power. Jim Griffiths was busy dismantling the British Empire and Stafford Cripps was also busy, inflicting austerity upon the nation. I was 30 miles north of Paris with a hard-earned and hard-saved £20 in my pocket. My passport carried Ernest Bevin's command to all foreign powers to allow me free passage without let or hindrance. I was 18, and with Ernie's assurance guaranteeing my well-being I intended to enjoy myself.

My original idea had been to spend two or three weeks touring a little around France, but these plans had been made before I had seen Paris or met with the mademoiselles of Montmartre. My stay in Paris proved to be much shorter than I had planned. I only had time to marvel at the well-known landmarks, stare in amazement at the well-stocked food markets, goggle at the pastries wallowing in cream in the gleaming windows of the patisseries, buy some chocolate for my chocoholic mother, who, poor soul, was still suffering under the agonies of rationing, before my savings finally evaporated in Pigalle. Broke, I was obliged to turn homewards within a week

5

of my arrival in Calais. Down to a few remaining francs, I spent the last night in Calais at a dingy waterfront hotel. This ancient construction was not only suffering from years of neglect but the numerous bombardments to which it had been subject during the war had added significantly to its overall decrepitude. It leaned dangerously on its foundations. However, given the state of my finances there was really no other alternative for a bed.

A quick inspection of my bedroom and its surrounds was sufficient for me to understand that washing facilities were non-existent and that other natural needs would be catered for by the provision of the usual hole in the ground located somewhere in the immediate area of the hotel. Dropping my haversack on the bed, I descended to the bar and remained there until well into the early morning. Then, suffused with a warm alcoholic glow and to the accompaniment of 'Tipperary' being hammered out by a very dunken pianist, I carefully navigated the uncarpeted wooden staircase back to my bedroom. The last sounds I heard as I opened the door to my room was a shout from the bar followed by the crash of a piano lid and then there was silence. Presumably the remaining occupants of the bar had had enough of the pianist. I did not sleep well. The bed sloped with the floor, which itself sloped in harmony with the rest of hotel, and I was frequently deposited on the floor. In the morning I took the ferry back to England, bewitched by Paris and wanting to see something more of France. I made up my mind that I would return the next year.

In the years that followed that first visit I did return frequently, each time on a motorcycle and each time intending to see more of France. It never happened. Paris was an overwhelming attraction to me and I would stay north of the city near to Carrefour Pleyel in an *Aux Routiers*. This establishment consisted of a two-storey building containing a café on the ground floor, while the upstairs rooms provided living space for 'le patron' and his family. At the back was a single-storey outhouse which had been converted into half a dozen bedrooms. They were clean, equipped with washbasins, and

6

for the princely sum of 4 francs a night I could stay there for bed and breakfast and then spend the rest of my time and money in Paris. It was a good, cheap base where I could leave the bike and make excursions into the city by bus and metro, and I used it each year that I came to Paris. That is, until the day I was thrown out.

On that particular trip I was accompanied by Gordon, riding pillion. Gordon was a close friend of my student days. Tall and gangly, honest and reliable, he was the product of a good British public school of that era. He was, of course, completely sex-starved, as most of us were at that time. The easy sex of the sixties was still ten years or more ahead of us. I was fond of Gordon, although by today's standard he would probably have been classified as a bit of a wimp. This wimpishness, which he combined with a general tendency to land himself into difficulties with apparent ease, made me feel largely responsible for him and so I was rather concerned when one night I lost track of him somewhere in a brothel around Gare St Lazare. I had last seen him entering a room of a dubious hotel accompanied by a pneumatic blonde, after which he had gone, so to speak, off the radar. It was well after midnight, and as I had the key to our *Aux Routiers* bedroom in my pocket, I realised that even if he could find his own way back, which I doubted, he would be stranded like a lost soul outside on the pavement. Anxiously I set about looking for him, but although a search among numerous bedrooms of the dubious hotel had revealed some amazing sights, there was no sign of Gordon. I was not and am still not kinky, and although voyeurism held no attractions for me I did eventually become interested in the sexual contortions which were being unfolded before my fairly innocent eyes at each room I entered. Eventually my explorations landed me into trouble and I was firmly escorted out into the street and told to go away by a heavily built gentleman who expressed no interest whatsoever in the possible whereabouts of Gordon.

Worried, I began to make my way back to the *Aux Routiers* and was fortunate enough to catch the last metro heading north out of Gare St Lazare. Upon arrival at Carrefour Pleyel,

7

I made my way to the bus terminal, only to be informed by a passing gendarme that it was pointless to wait at a bus stop at 1.30 in the morning because the next bus was not scheduled for at least another five hours. There was no alternative to walking the rest of the way if I wanted to have a bed for what remained of the night. This task would have been facilitated if I had known the exact address of the *Aux Routiers*, but unfortunately all that I remembered was that it was located somewhere on the road between Carrefour Pleyel and Amiens. Helped by directions as to the route for Amiens given to me from every late-night passer-by, and no longer concerned about Gordon but determined to strangle him if I ever did find him, I eventually arrived and opened the door to our room. Gordon was in bed, apparently sleeping peacefully, with a beatific smile of sexual contentment illuminating his face. Awakened by my kick and accompanying strong words, he pleaded with me to be calm because he had something serious to tell me. I restrained my desire to twist his neck and listened as he went on to explain that we had a problem. Being keyless, he had climbed in through a window. 'Good thinking,' I remarked, and so it had been – except that he had mistakenly chosen a room occupied by two Swedish girls both asleep in their beds. Awakened by the sight of Gordon's ungainly body clumsily approaching them and unable to understand his inebriated 'Scuse me, ladies', they had both screamed piercingly and continually in unison. Apparently the police had just left when I arrived and the following morning the proprietor asked us to find other accommodation. Such is life.

Eventually on one holiday I did manage to get as far as Le Mans to see the 24-hour road circuit and, imagining that I was taking part in a race, succeeded in losing my wallet, which had probably fallen from my pocket as I negotiated a particularly difficult corner. I was amazed when some weeks later it was returned by the local police, complete with papers and money, to my home in Liverpool. Times were different then.

All my memories of those wild, youthful visits to Paris are happy ones. The beauty of the architecture as well as the girls impressed me, even though most of the buildings were badly

8

in need of cleaning, as I suppose were some of the girls. Lunching on the bank of the Seine with a baguette, cheese and a bottle of *vin ordinaire*. The dense, noisy traffic of the Champs-Elysées with the motorists continually sounding their horns. That early morning Paris smell of freshly baked bread and coffee which filled the air while workmen washed and besomed the streets. The *joie de vivre* apparent in the cafés. The pace and the excitement of life in the city. Paris with its blue skies. Paris with its bustle. The left bank, Montmartre, Place de la Concorde. City of light, City of life. Paris pulsated. Paris was something. I was in love with it.

2

PARIS VIA BELFAST

Years later I was struggling to earn a living as an engineer in the Britain of Harold Wilson. He who was going to build a new Britain, not only based upon the usual political promises of a better social justice with prosperity for all being just around the corner, but also upon meritocracy. Amongst all his promises the reference to meritocracy inspired me the most and I mentally assured Harold that he would most certainly have my support. In the Britain of those days the mention that one was an engineer was usually met with such expressions as: 'Oh! So you're an engine driver then,' or alternatively: 'Are you any good at car repairs because mine has just developed a slight knocking noise and I wonder if the big end is going?' However, it was not just the confusion in the mind of the average Brit between a qualified engineer and an engine driver or mechanic, honourable though these professions are, which disillusioned me. The last straw was the pay. An engineer's salary at that time was pretty abysmal and in all probability both the engine driver and the mechanic were, with a little bit of overtime, receiving a higher remuneration than a qualified engineer.

Sometime later, Harold's assurance that the devalued pound in my pocket was still worth a pound failed to interest me. My problem was the scarcity of pounds in my pocket regardless of their relative value. It was the search for more pounds in my pocket which finally led me away from the stress of producing hydraulic gearboxes and similar complicated devices into the aseptic world of custard powder. Strange though it may seem, despite the fact that the engineering technology required for such an activity was, and perhaps still is, considerably less, the

10

pay was, and perhaps still is, considerably better. Engineers in the 1960s could find higher-paid jobs in the pharmaceutical and food industries than in the world of light or heavy engineering. So I joined a food company.

The salary afforded a better standard of living but I did find it difficult to relate to custard. Previously I had worked in the relatively rough world that was then associated with the production of agricultural and automobile equipment. This was in the days before computer control had sanitised the industry and the shop floor was still filled with plump little ladies with curlers peeping from beneath their turbans. They made their capstan lathes sing in tune to *Music While You Work* as they produced component parts to a piecework rhythm. The production managers and foremen of the epoch were a fairly hard-bitten crew and most of them had gradually worked their way into management from the shop floor. They were rich in experience and vocabulary if somewhat light in diplomas. I had changed this world for one of young newly qualified graduates who were straight from the universities. Dressed in impeccable white coats and paper hats, they circulated politely like acolytes among the open plan offices and the gleaming stainless steel tanks of a vast cathedral dedicated to the glory of custard. I may have become richer but I was in danger of becoming bored rather rapidly.

It was the swinging sixties. A time when unemployment along with the Wars of the Roses belonged to the history books. The space age was upon us. Austerity was behind us and there was an optimistic belief in future economic growth. Despite the few management gurus who advised a policy of 'stick to the knitting', many industries were engaged in a rush of expansion through horizontal integration, believing that if they could successfully manage in one industry they could do the same in any other they considered similar. The company I worked for was no exception and the opportunity to relieve my boredom presented itself when my employers launched into the manufacture of pet food. Reflecting the optimism of the time, they decided to pursue this activity, operating out of a Northern Ireland base, and I was asked if I would join a

11

small task force to work in their newly acquired factory in Armagh. Given the trouble that was brewing in Northern Ireland in 1970, the deal was that we, the task force of three, would take the early 'red eye' flight to Belfast each Monday and return to the safety of our own homes each Friday evening. Weekday accommodation in Northern Ireland was to be provided for us in a small hotel at company expense.

Happy to escape from the routine of custard and similar products, I agreed to the proposition and was soon amongst the mud and the blood of Northern Ireland helping to make canned dog food. The Irish are a wonderful people to work with, and although I wondered at first why it was that all the managers were Protestants and all the production workers were Catholic, there was so much to do that I did not have too much time to spare for such thoughts. There were difficulties however, notably the activities of the IRA. Late in the evening I would be luxuriating in a Badedas scented hot bath trying to rid myself of the smell of animal fat and vainly waiting for the naked woman on a white horse to appear at the bathroom window in line with the advertisements of that epoch. These adverts promised that 'Things happen when you take a Badedas bath'. The only thing that happened to me was to be notified of a bomb alert in the factory. I would then be obliged to leave the comfort of a hot bath, throw on some clothes and hurry to the factory in the cold dismal Irish night, not that there was much I could do when I arrived there, except evacuate the place and call up the army to search among the pallets of canned dog food. Looking for a bomb in a canning factory can only be compared to searching for the proverbial black cat in a dark room, at night.

The events surrounding Bloody Sunday and its aftermath did not help the situation either. One subsequent morning, with the whole of Northern Ireland strike-bound, I was advised by the police to shut the factory down and allow all the personnel to return to their homes. Having done this, and checked that the factory was empty and secured, I thought that my best plan would be to get the hell out of there myself. Given that all Ulster's exit ports were closed and that

12

Northern Ireland had suddenly become isolated from the rest of the world, I reckoned that my escape route back to England and sanity probably lay in borrowing the company's bullet-holed Ford and heading across the border to Dublin airport. It was not an easy journey as barricades were being built across the roads and weird-looking men, complete with balaclavas and pick handles, were roaming the streets looking very unpleasant and ferocious. Armagh in general was gradually becoming equivalent to a pain in the left chest so far as I was concerned. Still, if nothing else, life was not boring and I found it preferable to a return to the world of custard powder.

The work I did in Ireland seemed to satisfy the company. It was not that I was a particularly good engineer, but before the purchase the factory had been a family business and run very much as a one-man show, or rather as a one-man show might have been run at the turn of the century. A fairly heavy investment programme was necessary and major changes to working practices required if the business was to compete in the market place. In fact the factory was an industrial engineer's paradise and anything I did had to be an improvement on the previous situation. The Irish workforce proved to be pleasant and co-operative, so it was not difficult for me to be seen to be achieving satisfactory results, at least so far as the managers back in England were concerned. This was good news as they held the key to any future opportunities that I might be lucky enough to have offered to me, and it was probably due to the fairly good reputation I built up during the two years I spent in Ireland that decided the company to offer me the chance of an international transfer. An offer which would require me to work and live in Paris. I was overjoyed, and it was not only the warm feeling which I had always retained for France and particularly for Paris which persuaded me to accept the offer. The transfer to the French subsidiary not only offered Paris but also my salary would be doubled. I accepted with alacrity. Who wouldn't?

To live in France

In 1972 the removal of the family and our belongings from a Cotswold village to France and the early days of our residence there were chaotic. The French subsidiary had found a house for rent in the Parisian suburb of Neuilly-sur-Marne which they considered to be suitable for the family, which then included, as well as my wife Heather and myself, our two adolescent daughters, Jane and Ann, three cats and an Alsatian dog. It was, they told us, difficult to find houses for rent in the Paris area and an apartment would obviously be unsuitable for our menagerie. Digesting this news, Heather and I made a one-day trip over to view and agree the house, and the company then entered into a rental contract for the property on our behalf. Jane and Ann, at 16 and 14 years of age respectively, were thrilled by the idea of the move, and an air of excited anticipation pervaded the whole family. It was only much later that I fully realised the trauma I had subjected the family to in lifting them from a quiet Cotswold village and plunging them into the pressures of life in Paris.

This was in the days before the UK became a member of the European Community, and foolishly I had depended upon the UK company's personnel department to attend to the formalities attached to the transfer of the family, furniture and other possessions to a foreign location. In was only later, with painful experience gathered the hard way, that I realised that they were virtually as unfamiliar with what to do in this sort of affair as I was. One of our main problems, at least so far as UK officialdom was concerned, was centred around the animals, and this involved us in a number of trips to the Ministry of Agriculture and Fisheries in London. There were horrendous veterinary bills to pay for various certificates and other miscellaneous papers until finally we were equipped with a dossier some 2 inches thick containing sufficient licences, veterinary reports and certificates to satisfy any demanding immigration officer who showed an interest in our travelling zoo.

14

The animals apart, it took us weeks of work to make the required detailed inventory of the furniture and other household items and to obtain all the supposed necessary documentation. Each licence, paper, list and document was painstakingly arranged into its respective dossier and I purchased a briefcase specifically for their safekeeping and transportation. Our furniture was shipped off in advance and finally, one chilly morning in October 1972, we loaded up our second-hand Cortina to the roof-rack with pots and pans, bedclothes and other items which we considered to be immediate essentials, and with the children, the dog and the three cats aboard headed for Dover.

Disembarking in Calais, nervous but confident that our impressive collection of documents would meet all the requirements of the strictest immigration control, I inched the car forward in the queue towards the passport barrier. The smartly dressed immigration officer looked incredulously at the car and its occupants. Gazing curiously at the mattress tied to the roof rack, and the dog, cats and children jumbled on the back seat he probably thought that it was just his luck to meet with a load of nomads in transit. It may have been because he was tired or nearing the end of his shift but for one reason or another he evidently decided that the heap of bedclothes and kitchen equipment on wheels was just too much for him. Glancing briefly at our passports and looking deadpan at the car once more, he remarked 'English, eh! You're not smuggling cornflakes, are you?' Then, chuckling to himself over his little joke, he waved us on. We were in France. We had wasted a lot of effort, time and money collecting documents in England. They looked impressive and I felt a little hurt that he did not even want to look at them. In time I was to learn that the French had sufficient dossiers of their own and were not in the market for importing them from England or anywhere else.

The rest of the journey to Paris was uneventful and upon arrival we unloaded the car at the house. Our furniture, however, had not arrived and frantic calls to the removal company revealed that it had been shipped to Switzerland in error, which seemed an ominous start to our new life. We left

15

the animals at the house with food and access to the garden, and the human members of the family booked into a nearby hotel. We were to stay there for a week or so until the various customs officers and transport companies concerned unravelled the problem and our furniture was finally delivered.

Paris was still the Paris I remembered. True, the city now seemed to have a greater sense of urgency. New buildings and new roads were under construction. Everywhere huge cranes towered over the rooftops and to the west reared the sky scrapers of La Défense. Right bang in the centre of the city, or so it seemed, the black obelisk of Montparnasse raped the skyline. Suburbs had grown and Neuilly-sur-Marne presented a panorama of new high-rise apartment blocks, with many still under construction. Paris itself though was little changed. Its centre never slept. Traffic still coursed along the 'Champs' at three o'clock in the morning and by seven o'clock was intense. The cafés and bakeries were already open by then, the streets being washed. The metro disgorged workers and people were thronging the streets at a much earlier hour than I had been used to seeing in England. Hanging over all this activity was that early morning Parisian smell of fresh bread and coffee, which brought back my happy memories of student holidays.

Our hotel was to the east of Paris on Le Cours de Vincennes, and twice a week a street food market sprang up overnight and stretched the few hundred yards to the Place de la Nation. There is nothing more Parisian than the street market. Its colour, its smells, its noise and its characters. The Frenchwomen seemed to throw themselves whole-heartedly into the act of buying in a market. They displayed a knowledge of the produce which I had never seen exercised in England. They would sniff at a melon to judge its ripeness, examine each fruit and vegetable carefully and scrutinise each cheese, delicately feeling the texture of a Camembert between finger and thumb before concluding any purchase. Saturday mornings we would stroll the length of the market, not to purchase anything but to marvel at the range of fruit and vegetables, arranged in such a way that the colours harmonised, making

16

each stall a visual delight. The French we found were artists at presentation. A glance into the windows of any florist's revealed magnificent displays of flowers carefully arranged and bright with colour, which contrasted strongly with the local flower shops back home, where they usually displayed bunches of drooping daffodils in a galvanised bucket labelled 'Daffs 25p a bunch'. The children especially were delighted by the displays of candy in many of the *confiseries*, where sweets wrapped in contrasting colours of red or blue or white and arranged into complex patterns looked tempting and expensive. Purchase of these sweets revealed the latter to be true, but after the wrapping paper was removed one was faced with a mundane boiled sweet, confirming my growing belief that the French could make the most ordinary objects look luxurious.

In the early morning the cafés were crowded, firstly with workmen taking a breakfast of coffee and croissants, smoking their Gauloises and some taking a small white wine. Later came the office workers repeating the same performance and all these smells of coffee and Gauloises and croissants mingled with the street smells to produce an exciting mix peculiar to Paris.

In 1972 the café not only served as a centre for refreshment and discussion, it was also virtually the only place where one could find a telephone or a lavatory – and with Gallic indifference these two activity centres were usually located in close proximity to each other. This made telephoning rather a public affair as a constant stream of lavatory users shouldered their way past the telephone, and the caller's conversation was occasionally punctuated by the noise of flushing water. The lavatories themselves showed little improvement on the one I had encountered long ago in a small *auberge* somewhere near Amiens. Most of them were modelled '*à la turque*'. For the uninitiated, a lavatory *à la turque* consists of a shallow, rectangular ceramic basin about three feet square, recessed into the floor. In the centre is an open drain hole, a convenient distance from which two raised ceramic footprints indicate where to put one's feet. In these contrivances flushing was, to say the

17

least, perilous. One pull on the lever and a tidal wave hit your feet, soaking your socks. This phenomenon probably explained why many people refrained from any flushing activity whatsoever, preferring to leave the place as rapidly as possible, with an every man for himself attitude. To add to an Englishman's embarrassment, the French café owners with their cavalier attitude to the basic functions of the human body saw no reason to provide separate facilities for women, and I still wonder how they managed with an '*à la turque*'. I felt for them. Heather avoided *à la turque* lavatories like the plague, and I could only assume that French women had developed unusually strong thigh muscles to enable them to stand on the footprints and squat over the drain. Fortunately for all concerned, this type of toilet arrangement has now almost disappeared in France.

Use of the phone required a token, which was bought from the café proprietor, and I always felt that I had to buy at least one coffee before asking for one, a practice which substantially added to the cost of telephoning. The telephone system itself was something else. In fact at that time, with the exception of international calls, the French telephone system hardly worked at all. Once established and working in one of the company's offices, I found it quicker to relay a telephone message from Paris to Reims via an international call to England rather than to try to get through internally in France.

In the rest of the café a certain standard of hygiene was observed, but a hygiene with its roots in agricultural France and not in bacteria-conscious Britain. Cups were invariably clean although frequently cracked, flies on the croissants were accepted with tolerance. Cigarette ash was dropped on the floor, as were cigarette ends, there to be ground out underfoot. Elsewhere in the street the agricultural approach to hygiene made itself evident in the meticulous care taken in clearing away the debris at the close of the street markets, and the effective street washing, while the nearby street *pissotières* were ignored, as it was the habit of a great number of Frenchmen to urinate against the nearest tree. I concluded that these were not necessarily a dirty people but that they

18

differed from the English in that they saw the natural bodily functions for what they are, natural.

Our few days in the hotel ended and I began to attend a language school on the Left Bank, where I was to learn basic conversational French over a six-week period, My previous exposure to the language had been at school many years ago and had remained at the *Où est la plume de ma tante* level. The lessons at the Left Bank school were good, and had I been allowed to finish the six-week course I might have acquired a reasonable working knowledge of the language. However, because of an urgency the company called me back to work after I had only completed two weeks of the course, and that was the end of my language tuition. The rest of my French was to be picked up over time in the various factories I would be working in. Nevertheless, the two weeks of lessons that I did complete allowed me to ask directions, purchase items in shops and so on. Years later I reminded the company of their debt to me of a further four weeks' tuition and they, obligingly, arranged for me to meet with a French professor to assess my actual level. This gentleman, after listening to me speak for a few minutes, shook his head, murmured '*Mon Dieu*' and '*Mon pauvre*' and said that my only hope was to forget all that I had learned and start again. I did not have the courage to do that, which was something I was later to regret.

Who are you, exactly?

It was at this time that my first real exposure to French bureacracy began. I needed a work permit. This was to mean frequent visits to the prefecture, to which I was accompanied, thankfully, by Jean Claude, one of the company's personnel managers who, having a working knowledge of English, acted as my interpretor, my own French being hopelessly inadequate for the occasion. During the first visit, when after about a two hours' wait it was finally our turn to approach the counter and be dealt with, I became aware of many shakings of the head, shrugs and other generally negative gesticulations. I was asked through my interpreter to produce my English identity card, my *livret de famille* and my health certificate. A *livret de famille* is a small booklet issued to marrying couples after the obligatory civil ceremony. It contains basic information (names, dates, etc.) that relate to the couple's parents and to themselves. Details of any children are entered into the booklet at the time the births are registered. Unfortunately, as I tried to explain, I did not possess any of these items as none of them existed in the UK. Up to now, I pointed out, the British had got by in general with only a birth certificate, a marriage licence, a passport and eventually a death certificate. I added that while it was true that during the war I had been issued with an identity card, my mother had burned it, along with those of the rest of the family as soon as the war ended. I could remember that my wartime identity number had been NIEP 61–4 if that was any use. This information did not appear to interest the official, who, apart from requesting that Jean Claude repeat the part about my mother burning the family's identity cards and appearing to view this as a sacrilege equal to defacing the Bible, began to show signs of impatience. Eventually, after much discussion he appeared to resign himself to accepting that the English were akin to the Martians, and I was told that as a first step I must present myself for a medical examination at the approved medical centre.

Explaining the situation to me, Jean Claude pointed out, to my consternation, that I was completely outside the law as I could not rent a house before I had a work permit, but that I could not have a work permit before I had an address, and obviously I could not work in France without a work permit. I interjected at this stage, in the interest of cultural exchange to tell him that this sort of situation is known in England as a 'catch 22', after the novel by Joseph Heller. Unimpressed by my literary knowledge, Jean Claude neatly summed up the situation by telling me that the problem was that I was not allowed to work in France; but I was doing so. I was also renting a house and that was also illegal. Furthermore, he concluded, my birth certificate was of no use whatsoever as it was written in English and was more than six months old. I

20

mentioned that I was also more than six months old and that in Britain you were only issued with one birth certificate, normally when you were born. Furthermore, I added, that it was normal for my birth certificate to be written in English because I happened to have been born in an anglophone country. This information was met by Jean Claude with a movement of his shoulders expressively dismissing all things British as beyond the pale, while the expression on his face could only have been translated into English to mean 'My God! I've got a right one here'.

Finally wheels were set in motion for my medical examination The actual examination was to my mind a complete waste of time. It took place in the rue de Vaugirard in south Paris and I was asked to present myself there at eight o' clock one particular morning. I arrived at the appropriate metro station and easily located the centre because there were about 300 other people of various nationalities and colours waiting outside in the street. When eventually about an hour later the doors of the medical centre were opened, everybody tried to be the first in and in the ensuing charge some were left behind jammed in the doorway while others were incapacitated from blows delivered from aggressive elbows. Many probably left as walking wounded in a far worse state of health than that in which they had arrived. In my particular case I felt that if I could get from Neuilly-sur-Marne or any other eastern suburb to rue de Vaugirard in southern Paris for eight in the morning, wait in the street for an hour and survive the ensuing charge when the doors had finally opened, I had to be in the best of health. Most of the other people had probably undergone a similar trial and I thought that the French government could have saved a considerable amount of money by just taking everybody's name and address and then sending them straight home again as obviously nothing much could be wrong with them.

Eventually I received a medical certificate stating I was in good physical health, although any examination of my mental state would have identified that I was on the verge of a nervous breakdown, so it was back to the préfecture. It was a

21

fruitless journey as further information concerning my grandmother's maiden name was requested and I was not able to say whether or not my grandmother had even been married, although I had always assumed that she had been. This failed to impress oficialdom and we came away without the papers we required. I was still illegal. About this time I seriously considered giving up and going home to a culture that I understood, but persevered, being nothing if not tenacious. Eventually I suspected that I was involved in a sort of game, the rules of which were simply that if I obtained the paper I came for the official was the loser. If I did not obtain it and had to come back because I did not have all the necessary supporting documents, then the official had won.

Following many failures I finally became adept at this game. The secret to winning was not to show my hand. I learned never, but never, to put all my supporting documents on the counter at the beginning of the game. I pretended that I had none. This lulled the official into a false sense of security and he became overconfident. 'Have you,' he might ask with a smugly condescending air, 'your updated birth certificate?' I would immediately pull the necessary certificate from out of my breast pocket and say innocently, 'Do you mean this?' The official would become crestfallen and I found that, on average, if I applied the same technique to the next three items that he demanded, he would realise that he was playing the game with a professional, look at me with some respect and almost certainly give me the paper I had come for without further ado, accepting with Gallic grace that this time he was the loser. So with time and tenacity I became legal. Shortly after, Great Britain joined the European Community and I no longer needed a work permit. Well, you can't win them all.

Meanwhile, on the domestic side we were settling in well. My wife and the children attended the Alliance Française to learn French. The Alliance Française is a government-sponsored association aimed at extending French influence by the teaching of the French language. The standard of teaching is good, and the fees low. Later the children attended the local lycée. We were fortunate in having as a next-door neighbour one of the kindest gentlemen I have ever known. He was a tremendous help to us in settling down. In fact all our neighbours were helpful and even welcoming in a cautious manner. I was surprised that our friendly neighbour, who frequently invited us over to his house either for a drink or to watch television, always addressed me as Monsieur. He proved to be a gentleman in every sense of the word and would go to endless trouble in helping us out with any domestic problem, be it with the plumbing or the telephone or ordering fuel or whatever. I would have liked to become more friendly with him but his insistence in calling me Monsieur inhibited me from any closer contact. He was hospitalised for a short time with a relatively minor illness and I visited him. It was the first time that I had been inside a French hospital and I was surprised when he opened his bedside locker, pulled out a bottle of red wine and offered me a glass. I could not have imagined such an act being tolerated in an English hospital.

We stayed in the house at Neuilly for nearly four years and our neighbour and I continued calling each other Monsieur for all that time. My children, who were making great strides in French, told me that I should use the '*tu*' pronoun instead of '*vous*' when talking to them or indeed to other close friends. This difference in the second person pronoun does not exist in English if we ignore the poetic use of 'thou', and I found it very confusing. I began *tu*'ing instead of *vous*'ing and obviously often caused surprise and alarm to various people in the course of a day. In business I decided to use *tu* to everybody working in my department, and this was accepted, although I was warned by one of the engineers, for reasons he could not or would not explain, that I should not use *tu* to my secretary.

Towards the end of my first year in France I began to acclimatise to living there, although many facets of the life were still puzzling. I was still a long way from understanding French mentality and was confused by the contrasts that surrounded me daily. The aggression of drivers on the road contrasted with the politeness and formality I met with socially. The well-kept houses and gardens of the suburbs were in contrast to the general untidiness of the streets. It was as if

23

the Frenchman was saying to the world at large 'I am proud of my garden and the looks of my house; what happens in the street outside my garden gate is not my concern.' The French seemed to me to be strongly individualist, with little sense of community or team spirit. I had not yet become aware of the extreme generosity and support given by the French when faced with a request from a charitable organisation. I wondered how it could be that two peoples, the French and the British, could be such close geographical neighbours, share so much of the same basic European culture and yet be so different in their daily lives. I was convinced that those 22 miles of Channel had to be the longest 22 miles that ever existed.

3

PIERRE AND FELIPE

I was in the chewing gum business. The French, I discovered, chewed a lot of gum. GI Joe had apparently left a little bit of his culture behind him. So far as the company I was now working with was concerned, equipped as they were with three factories and a total of over 1,000 people on the payroll, it was big business. It all added up to a lot of gum to be finally spat out on the pavements or to end its days stuck under some inoffensive restaurant table. Although the company did manufacture some other confectionery lines, notably candy and bubblegum, chewing gum was the mainstay of the business. All these were products of which I had no experience and, given the trauma of settling the family in a new country and trying to learn the language, things generally were pretty sticky all round.

I was placed under the care of the chief engineer, Pierre, who allocated me an office in the technical centre of the largest chewing gum factory. Pierre was a living caricature of a stage Frenchman. Excitable, small and round with a Louis Napoleon beard, he lacked only a beret and a baguette stuck under his arm to complete the picture. Despite his excitability he was a shy man, and although in character with most French managers of that time he was light on human relations and communication, he was, I discovered, technically a very competent engineer. On my first day as a new boy in his department he escorted me to my office, which turned out to be one of many located along a lengthy corridor in the technical centre. Opening the door he proudly showed me the empty desk and bare walls, and then with a murmured wish that I would find everything to my liking, left me, shutting the door behind him. This business of shutting office doors and keeping them closed I found later to be a frequently occurring phenomenon in the French style of management. It is intimidating. There is nothing as effective as a long silent corridor of closed doors for striking a feeling of uncertainty and loneliness in the heart of any stranger unfortunate enough to find himself in unfamiliar territory.

Left alone, I decided that I would at least find out where the washroom was situated, a minor although relatively important feature in any establishment and a detail which Pierre had neglected to show me. Leaving my office with the door open so that I would be able to recognise it when I returned, I explored the corridor. Eventually I found not only the washroom but the stairs that led to the canteen and the door that led into the factory yard. In fact I made quite a tour of the factory without meeting with any complication except that upon eventually finding my way back to the technical centre and its long corridor of offices, I discovered somebody had closed my office door. Like cats at night, all closed office doors look the same, and there was no alternative but to knock on the nearest door. Using the fruits of my two-week French course, I introduced myself to the occupant as the new Industrial Engineering Manager and, feeling stupid, asked if the occupant knew which was my office. He didn't, and the resulting confusion led us inevitably back to Pierre, who once more escorted me to my office and once more left me there, once more shutting the door behind him as he departed.

Feeling really intimidated, I decided against venturing out on a second sortie. I passed the time arranging a couple of pencils and a new writing pad on my desk, and when that was done I opened and examined the drawers of my empty filling cabinet. Neither of these tasks proved very time-consuming and so I finally sat down at my pristine desk and deflowered the writing pad with a letter home to Mum. The afternoon dragged on. I had not been advised of normal working hours and indeed there didn't seem to be any. It was approaching seven in the evening when Pierre put his head around my door to wish me 'Bonsoir'. His departure produced similar results

26

to those of a school bell at the end of the day and all hell broke loose. The technical centre became immediately alive with shouted '*Bonsoirs*' and the sound of the hurrying footsteps of engineers and secretaries making full speed for the door. Evidently everybody worked the same hours as Pierre.

It was fortunate for me that my real boss was the Production Director, Felipe. But it was unfortunate for both of us that he was located in the head office on the other side of Paris, which rather complicated any communication between the two of us. However, he did at least set me a work programme. Felipe was a flamboyant Spaniard and a most remarkable man. Educated as an engineer, he had passed through the stages of industrial engineering to become a factory manager and then a director. Later on in his career he was to become general manager in another company and then later to move into even higher spheres of management. I didn't know it then but he was to change my life completely, and I was to meet with him and to work with him again in the years ahead.

Felipe had charisma and working for him was a pleasure once I became used to his explosive temperament. On one occasion when he was due to participate in a particularly difficult meeting with the visiting American management, he asked me to be on standby and to remain in his office in case he wished for any reason to call me into the meeting. I was relieved when he did not need my services but I realised that the meeting must have been a tough one when around midday Felipe stormed back into his office, stood directly facing me and began to shout loudly. He saw the look of amazed terror on my face and apologised immediately. 'I forget that you are English,' he said. 'You don't understand. I am Spanish and right now I need to shout, but I am not shouting at you. I am sorry. I will shout out of the window.' He walked across his office, flung open the window and yelled in Spanish over the rooftops of Paris. Then he turned to me and said, 'Now I feel better.' This was Felipe, and the glimpses of human warmth that he frequently showed, coupled with his intellectual brilliance, made him one of those very rare characters, a leader that people would follow anywhere.

27

One day when we were together it occurred to me to ask him why he had chosen to employ me. 'Well,' he had replied, 'I needed an anglophone engineer. Of course I really would have preferred an American but they are so expensive. You British are so cheap.' Felipe was nothing if not frank.

'By indirections find directions out'
William Shakespeare: *Hamlet*

The business was expanding and part of my job consisted of evaluating the industrial-equipment needs for the factories and then to prepare requests for capital investment. These requests were hopefully to be approved either by the European management located in Brussels or by even higher management located in the States, the approval level depending upon the amount of funds requested. I began to learn the intricacies of chewing gum and candy manufacture. Basically there is not really such a great deal of difference between making candy or dog food, or even custard for that matter. One puts ingredients in a mixer, mixes them, cooks them if necessary and then packages them in one form or another. The techniques of this sort of food processing can be learned by any reasonably intelligent person in about six months.

The first real difficulty I had to overcome lay not in the technology nor in grasping the essentials of the French language, but in translating French into English and then presenting it in the jargon that was comprehensible to an American businessman. Generally it was possible to translate two pages of French into one page of English and then finally condense it to half a page for American consumption. If this was difficult for me to do, it bordered on the impossible for a Frenchman, however good his knowledge of the English language. I began to realise why I had been employed as I became more and more witness to the way the Frenchman interweaves his love of debate with a philosophical approach to the solving of any work-associated problem. This intellectual contortion is then expressed through an indirect style of

28

communication, giving a final result that is capable of sending the average Anglo-Saxon to the brink of a total nervous collapse.

The love of debate manifested itself whenever a French manager attempted to present a project for approval by American management. In front of an impatient audience working against a tight time schedule and used to communication in the form of punchlines each of no more than half a dozen words, the Frenchman would initially outline the project's objective and scope. He would then painstakingly show all the details of the supporting study, explaining in depth the logic and the research supporting the project. It was only when all this had been demonstrated and the pros and cons carefully analysed at great length that the demand for the necessary funds was put on the table. This latter information was what the Americans had been waiting to find out since the beginning of the discourse, but long before the Frenchman had arrived at this crucial point the American and British managers present had fallen asleep. The final strain placed upon the shredded nerves of any stalwart American determined to keep a stiff upper lip and control his impatience at such a meeting came with the French use of indirect speech. The French are rarely direct. Perhaps they hope that indirect communication will give rise to the opportunity to engage further in their love of debate. Whatever the reason, questions asked would inevitably receive such answers as: 'Yes and no', or more positively: 'Yes, but. . . .' The Anglo-Saxon, who relies on direct communication, expects a binary response to his questions and equates indirectness with dishonesty. The Frenchman, from his point of view, equates directness with rudeness and consequently any attempt at serious communication between the two business cultures gets off to a bad start. Most of the meetings between French and Anglo-Saxons at which I assisted rapidly became difficult. I began to suspect that Felipe was not unduly concerned about my rather mediocre engineering skills. His concern was to have someone on his staff who could translate the tortuous verbosity of a French manager into the terse punchlines familiar to the American businessman.

'Yet meet we shall'
Samuel Butler: *Life after Death*

In the French company the customary first step to starting a project was to hold a preparatory meeting or *pré-réunion*. The purpose of this event was for a few select managers to decide whether or not a full meeting on the subject was necessary, and if so, what were the items to be discussed and who were the people who should attend. Then followed the stage of numerous meetings which the French management called whenever they felt it was necessary that they should be doing something. Such meetings were usually inconclusive, but as everyone enjoyed them the call for another one was always greeted as a good idea. 'It was a good meeting,' I often heard people say, despite the fact that nothing had been decided. A meeting was generally considered to have been good when the intellectual tone of the debate was challenging.

The French enjoyed having as many people as possible to enjoy the cut and thrust of a meeting, even though this always resulted in two or three meetings taking place simultaneously as different groups formed amongst the members and began to discuss the topic in question amongst themselves. The resultant cacophony was akin to a Chinese parliament in full spate. In the fullness of time, should everyone have arrived at an agreement, or should discussion around the same subject have begun to pall, the decision would be made to undertake a 'pre-study'. Progress reports on the pre-study gave ample opportunity for a further round of meetings, but eventually if all went well a 'full study' would be called for. The next step was to move to the 'pre-project', and upon completion of that the actual 'project' would be started. However, at any time during the many meetings which punctuated this entire process a manager might decide to challenge any of the assumptions made, on the basis that conditions had changed since the previous meeting. In this event it was necessary to revert to the first step and start all over again. However, even if they didn't arrive at the stage of actually doing the project, there had been plenty of intellectually demanding debate and everyone had great fun demonstrating their intelligence by identifying reasons why the project could not be undertaken.

The French are rarely punctual, either in their business or private lives. A business meeting called perhaps for 10 a.m. would find the meeting room empty at that time, with the sole exception of any disciplined Anglo-Saxon such as myself who had been requested to attend. Some ten minutes later the head of a French manager would appear around the door and then rapidly disappear again with a muttered: 'Meeting not started yet then.' This would be followed sometime later by a second head, which would enquire: 'Nobody here yet?' and then helpfully add: 'I'll go and find everybody then.' Whereupon the second head would also disappear. Eventually the heads would appear and then disappear with increasing frequency, and an inevitable interference pattern would result until two or even three heads could be sighted at the same time. It was then possible to retain most of them in one place and so enable the meeting to get under way. With a little experience, I was able to work out a simple formula for estimating the probable length of time which any meeting would endure. It consisted of allowing a full hour as a constant and then adding a further 20 minutes for each participant, so that the probable duration for a five-people meeting could be estimated at 2 hours 40 minutes. This formula disregarded completely the subject under discussion, which seemed to have little or no bearing on the time spent at the meeting. I found this simple rule of thumb a great help in planning my day.

'The march of intellect'
Robert Southey: *Colloquies on the Progress and Prospects of Society*

At every level above the most menial tasks the French approach to work appeared to me to be diametrically opposite to that of the average Englishman of the 1960s. My experience of that period was that generally the Englishman found no fun whatsoever in the subject of work and was motivated only by an all-consuming desire to finish with it as fast as possible so that he could spend the maximum of his time upon a more agreeable subject. Consequently although in the past I had found it sometimes difficult to motivate the Englishman to actually start work, when he did eventually start he was inclined to look for the most efficient way to complete the task, considering that he had more important things than work with which to occupy his time and his mind. The Frenchman, on the other hand, steeped in his agricultural culture considered work to be an integral part of life. Work to the Frenchman was a serious activity, *une raison d'être*, and he approached it as such, exercising all his intellectual powers, imbued as he was with philosophical reasoning.

In daily life as well as in the work context I had begun to realise that the French are obsessed by the need to be considered intelligent. This attribute does not carry the same weight in England where, to the contrary, intelligence is usually regarded with some suspicion. Questioned on his abilities the average Englishman will rarely list intelligence as one of them but will more probably offer efficiency, honesty or humour as his strengths, considering these attributes preferable and certainly more virtuous than intelligence. In an address to Rugby School the celebrated Dr Arnold once said, 'What we must look for here is: Firstly, religious and moral principles: Secondly, gentlemanly conduct: Thirdly, intellectual ability.' A point of view which was possibly shared by a large number of English public schools until well after the Second World War. While the religious and moral principle bit may have taken a hammering in the 150-odd years since these words were first spoken, the striving after intellectual ability still does not appear to be considered tremendously important by the average Englishman, although this is certainly less true for the Welsh and the Scots.

Living in France, however, one becomes very quickly aware of the word *con*. This word was neither taught nor explained to me during my few language learning sessions at the Left Bank school, but my French dictionary gives it two meanings: a vulgar term for the female sex organ, or a vulgar term describing great stupidity. In the latter meaning it is spelt *con* when referring to a masculine noun or *conne* when referring to a feminine noun. But that is not all. The English language is not rich in curse words and the anglophone, lacking picturesque speech, has to make do with a rather limited vocabulary of four-letter Anglo-Saxon words mainly referring to parts of the human body or to some of its less charming functions. These words have little meaning when taken out of context and are used as expletives conveying nothing except the user's general dissatisfaction with events. While there are words of a sexual derivation used in current, impolite English to signify stupidity they have not been exploited to the degree that the French have exploited *con*. For example they can call someone a *con*, meaning that he is a stupid fool, they can call a situation *con*, meaning that it is a stupid situation, they can request someone to stop their *connerie*, which means to stop acting stupidly, or they can even accuse a person or object of having *l'air con*, meaning they or it look stupid. Briefly, the French take a vulgar word and apply it across the board either as a noun or an adjective to denote the stupidity they disdain so much.

I believe that one of the worst social offences that can be committed against a Frenchman is to make him feel stupid. In his first contact with another person the Frenchman will set out to prove to himself that he is the more intelligent of the two and will only become relaxed when he is convinced that he has that superiority. This French need to be assured that they are the possessors of a superior level of intelligence can even become a weakness in that it is open to flattery.

I often wondered on the origins of this French obsession with intelligence and whether or not it is perhaps a product of their education with its strong accent on philosophy. However it is certain that one meets with it in one form or another on a daily basis. It is frequently manifested in that cerebral contortion which the French call their '*Système D*', or in other words,

'How to resolve a seemingly impossible problem through the use of superior intelligence'. Evidently, to demonstrate an ability to resolve a seemingly impossible problem it is necessary to have one to start with, and as a consequence life in France and particularly business life is fraught with problems. In the absence of any real problem the Frenchman will quickly invent one. There is a sort of two-way indemnity in this because either solving the imaginary or otherwise problem will demonstrate the intelligence of the solver, which means that virtually all problems are solved; alternatively, in the unlikely event of failure, it will only underline the immensity of the problem, which was obviously impossible to solve by human means in the first place. Therefore whatever the outcome, the Frenchman is left with the belief in his intelligence intact.

This superior intelligence syndrome may also go some way towards explaining why a normally polite, formal and considerate people become imbued with collective lunacy when they take to the roads. The car being an extension of self, the Frenchman considers that he drives intelligently and expects other road users, who by definition are less intelligent than he, to respect his superior driving skill. Should a fellow road user be unfortunate enough not to show this respect, he is immediately classified as a *con* and treated accordingly.

Despite the fact that the French are endowed with as much basic honesty as any other nation and perhaps even more than most, a challenge to their ingenuity will bring out the worst in them. The average Frenchman respects another man's right to earn his living and will usually be scrupulously honest in dealings with him. However, faced with an impersonal system requiring him to pay some of his hard-earned money, he changes completely. He may sit for an hour in a café, consume a number of drinks and not be given a bill, but he would probably not even consider leaving without paying. Yet he will contort his body by crawling or leaping over all sorts of obstacles so that he can travel on the Metro without a ticket. He likes to beat any system which he regards as a challenge to his ingenuity. The more complicated the system, the greater the challenge and the greater his satisfaction in reassuring himself of his intelligence when he beats it. The authorities concerned, on the other hand, are determined that they will not be taken for *cons* and increase the complication and control of their particular system. The end result is an army of suspicious officials employed at enormous cost vainly trying to stop a basically honest people from indulging in their favourite pastime: that of demonstrating that they are more intelligent than any system. The officials are wasting their time.

After 12 months of working in France I was in a deep culture shock. However, not only was I beginning to like the French and want to understand them, but it was also necessary that I reached some level of comprehension of their culture if I was to be accepted by them and make any success at all of my French career. There was even more to it than that as I also believed it to be a great pity to live and work in a different country without enriching oneself with an under-standing of its culture. Most of the Americans and indeed some of the British that I met in the course of my business life apparently did not share the same ambition. The Americans tended to live in a colony in the rather select Parisian suburb of St Cloud in a way reminiscent of colonials in the days of empire. They sent their children to the American school, attended the American church and if ill went to the American hospital. On the one or two occasions when we were invited to a party given by American colleagues, we found ourselves spending the evening amongst a jovial crowd of Americans with not a Frenchman in sight. I thought it a little lamentable to live this sort of lifestyle. These Americans would return to the States after a few years in France very little the wiser from their experience in a foreign country, which seemed to me to be a wasted opportunity.

Working and living in France, I wanted to profit from the occasion and broaden my mind with a full understanding of the French. To do this I believed that I had to try and think like a Frenchman, immerse myself in their culture as much as possible and become as French as I could. I had spent the first year of my life in France comparing most things French, with the exception of their food and wine, unfavourably with their

UK equivalent. I would frequently feel frustrated by the way they approached and handled daily mundane events, whether this was simply crossing a busy road, buying an aspirin, or going for a restaurant meal in the evening. Why? I would ask myself. Why do they not do these things in the way the British do? A way which was to my mind always simpler and invariably better. I began to wonder why I thought the way I did and the French thought differently. It was all, I supposed, a matter of culture.

4

CULTURE SHOCK

To quote Alvin Toffler: 'Culture shock is what happens when a traveller suddenly finds himself in a place where yes can mean no, where a fixed price is negotiable, where to be kept waiting in an outer office is no cause for insult, where laughter may mean anger'.

Certainly the culture shock that I was suffering from had not reached such a proportion, but it was sufficiently great to create a slight feeling of disorientation in my private life and a much greater one in my business life. I had two alternative ways of handling the situation. I could join in the thinking of the majority of the Anglo-Saxons that I came into contact with in business and treat the problem with a dismissive shrug, accepting that the French are impossible and that my way was the right way. The Americans were the champions in this line of thinking and in fact extended the same reasoning to the rest of the entire world. The English came a good second in this game, taking the same approach as the Americans but with a condescending smugness which avoided them from protesting as loudly as the Americans that they were always right. The Germans, of course, did everything by the book. The book being a German one.

The alternative was to try and understand why the French appeared to be so difficult, to my way of thinking. It was not, I reasoned, as if I was trying to integrate into an entirely different culture such as those I would have encountered had I moved to the Orient or to some North African country; after all, the British and the French are both Europeans. The English Channel, or La Manche, to give it its French name, divides the two countries by only a short distance of some 22

37

miles. Geographically we are close neighbours, and ever since the Norman conquest of Britain we have shared to some degree a common heritage. There seemed no reason why there should be a great gulf between the perceptions of the two peoples, and yet I was having a major problem in understanding French mentality.

The French for their part were most welcoming in their approach to me, as in fact they are to the majority of foreigners. I was to live in France for the next 26 years and during that time I would be exposed only twice to an unfriendly reaction stemming from my English nationality. One came from my French stepdaughter at the tender age of seven, who returning from school one afternoon informed her mother that she would never speak to me again because she had learned that day that the English had burned Joan of Arc. The second remark also concerned the 'Maid' but was in the business context and sprang from the lips of an excited marketing director during a heated disagreement between the two of us. Exasperated by my continual refusal to see things his way, he finally exploded: 'We have had trouble with you people since you burned Joan of Arc.' It was useless on both occasions for me to protest that it was not the English but the French who were responsible for lighting the fire under the poor girl. However, their remarks were more amusing than hurtful and I have never felt unwelcome in France because of my foreign nationality: which is probably more than could be said for any foreigner living in England.

The French with their love of self-criticism will spend hours in philosophical discussion on their attitudes to foreigners and will convince themselves that they are racists. They are not. Any racism which exists in France is usually aimed at specific North African ex-colonies and probably has political roots. There is no French equivalent for such derogatory words as dago, wop, nig-nog, Kraut, Argie, Frog, Chink etc., which can unfortunately be heard only too frequently in the UK. I was made welcome in France and it was for me to try to understand why French culture had produced a certain way of reasoning, and to bridge that understanding with my own reasoning, if I was to have a happy long-term career there.

Ignoring any cultural influences which may possibly be passed from generation to generation through our genes, it seems probable that the attitudes people have, the way they tend to think and the way they live depends to a large degree upon the culture they have inherited from their parents, their education and their friends. This imposed culture is itself derived from various sources, but amongst these, I believe, a nation's history, geography and religion must be dominant factors.

'The happiest nations have no history'
George Eliot: *The Mill on the Floss*

A slight knowledge of French history was sufficient to suggest to me that it alone was capable of inducing a degree of insecurity into the French psyche. The history of France does not make pleasant reading unless one is addicted to horror stories. Such a long saga of murder, mayhem and misrule would be difficult to match. The English monarchs of the Middle Ages were probably little if any better than their French counterparts but maybe they had an easier task. Their kingdom was not fragmented as France was nor was it situated on a continent with the shifting frontiers which such a geographical location entails. In comparison to France, or indeed to most European countries, the England of the fourteenth century had already reached relative stability. Feudalism was finished and the ground had been laid for the emergence of new social classes. Such terrors as the Black Death, the plague of the mid-fourteenth century with its death toll of well over 30 per cent, may have struck fear into the hearts of the English population as a whole but it did not result in the civil disorders to which it gave rise in France and Germany. During the following century the Wars of the Roses produced bloody battles between the nobility, but by and large the civil population of the countryside was not too involved in the struggle.

So far as the average peasant was concerned, life in England was in the main untroubled by conflict. It is true that those living in the border country may have been subject to sporadic incursions from the Scots, but such tribulations do not compare with the suffering of the French people at the hands of the English invaders.

Every schoolboy knows, if only partially, the turbulent history that kept France and England either at war or on the brink of conflict from 1066 up to the early years of the twentieth century. However, the English and French viewpoints differ in terms of these conflicts. After 1066, most of the earlier conflicts took place on French soil and the English were usually the victors, and perhaps not only because of the superior firepower of the English longbow but also because in their arrogance the French aristocracy considered war to be the province of the nobility and the foot soldier worthless. Scenarios such as that of Agincourt, where French knights fell in their hundreds beneath arrows fired by English archers, became a frequent feature in French–English conflict during the Middle Ages. However, it was the English who were the invaders, and English victories meant that it was the French people who suffered the atrocities. It may be pleasant to imagine the English soldier of that time as a chivalrous knight in shining armour and the archer as a sturdy, disciplined yeoman in a leather jacket crying 'God for Harry' etc., but the reality was different. The English yeoman came to France to burn, pillage and rape and to grab whatever riches he could for himself, and these objectives he savagely fulfilled in every village or town he came across.

Neither did it end with the Hundred Years War; the two countries continued fighting on and off on French soil until 1558, when England finally lost its last French possession: Calais. The rights and wrongs of these historical confrontations may be long forgotten and now immaterial, but the memory of the conflicts can linger on in the collective consciousness of a nation. Every nation writes its own history, and indeed every historian may even interpret historical events in a different manner. Joan of Arc may have been a saint for the French but for the English she was a witch. In modern times the 1940 British retreat from Dunkerque can become, for the British, almost a victory, and future politicians can call upon the nation to rekindle the spirit of Dunkerque when times are difficult. To the French, however, Dunkerque remains not just a defeat but also the time when Britain abandoned France. Neither interpretation takes into account all the issues which were at stake at that time, and this is true of all our popular historical beliefs.

The problem with history is that it forms a definite part of our culture without most of us having anything but the slightest knowledge of the subject. Football hooligans are able to tunelessly sing the chorus of 'Rule Britannia', probably without being able to name one naval battle and possibly only knowing Nelson as a character from *The Archers*.

Most of us glean our skimpy historical knowledge from our schooldays and from popular beliefs, both of which sources tend to relate a politically biased story based on a succession of kings and foreign battles, with God and righteousness usually on the side of the nation writing the history. My schooldays briefly taught me that it was Wellington who defeated Napoleon at the glorious battle of Waterloo and by doing so saved Europe from a dictator. It did not labour the fact that England and other European kingdoms, concerned by the rise of a Continental republic, had in fact waged war against Napoleon for a number of years using English gold to finance the armies of Austria, Russia and Germany, and that in effect the strongest English cavalry was gold from London. The Corsican upstart had to be stopped, otherwise meritocratic ideas might, to the consternation of European aristocracy, spread across the French frontiers. Neither did my school history book dwell overmuch on the role of Blücher in the aforesaid confrontation. Blücher, without whose timely aid Wellington would have fought, at best, an inconclusive battle if not a losing one.

I could easily understand that the historical relationship between the two countries could well have developed a

41

national feeling of mistrust among the French for the English, the same being true for the English perception of the French.

In more recent years France has been invaded and devastated three times by German invasion. In the war of 1870 a confident France saw Paris fall to the invaders. In the war of 1914 a large part of northern France was destroyed and almost 6 million French soldiers were either killed or wounded. During the Second World War the French government capitulated to the Germans in 1940 and the country was occupied.

Although one cannot generalise about a nation of some 60 million inhabitants, it is probably safe to say that regardless of whatever degree of importance one allocates to history in the building of a nation's culture, in the case of France it was likely to breed a degree of insecurity.

Revolution, like Saturn, might devour her children
Pierre Vergniaud, in A. de Lamartine: *Histoire des Girondins*

France, I discovered, is a country split by internal discord. A second glance at its history shows the French as a people apparently possessed with a predilection for auto-genocide. In recent history the nation has passed from greatness to humiliation and back to greatness and staggered from one revolution to another with an almost monotonous regularity. In the years 1789, 1830, 1848, 1871, 1940–44, 1968, Frenchmen indulged in the madness of either physically harming or just simply killing each other in the interest of politics. Taking just one example: the three months of the Paris commune in 1871 alone witnessed some 25,000 Parisians killed by their fellow countrymen.

However, the revolution of 1789 was not the origin of this murderous division in the soul of what is otherwise one of the most civilised nations on earth. Long before that the French had found an excuse for engaging in their national pastime of creating bloody mayhem. The last half of the sixteenth century had seen them busily slaughtering each other in religious wars between Catholics and Protestants, punctuated by horrific

42

massacres. During the reign of Henry IV, who was probably one of the most intelligent of all the fairly dismal parade of French kings, the Edict of Nantes brought a halt to the killing of Protestants and for a short period France, perhaps alone amongst other European countries, including England, had legislation which allowed a degree of religious tolerance. It was not to last. Following the assassination of Henry, the suceeding Catholic monarchs gradually eroded the freedom of religious rights given to the Protestants. It fell to Louis X1V to finally revoke the Edict of Nantes in 1685. A couple of years before that he had expelled the Jews from France. Louis X1V was not a great believer in tolerance, apparently. Anyway, that was the end of religious tolerance in France, at least for the next hundred years or so.

Although the blind stupidity of the ruling classes probably made it inevitable, it is doubtful that the French Revolution achieved as much for France as it did for the rest of Europe in showing them that the old order could be changed. On the contrary, nurtured by philosophers, it resulted in a government which had no previous political awareness and which spent most of its time in fruitless debates over human rights, only to have these supposed rights completely ignored in the months to come. As in most revolutions, the intellectuals were rapidly disposed of and were superceded by fanatical tyrants. These psychopaths then plunged France into a reign of terror the like of which had never before been witnessed in a civilised western European nation. Europe was to wait another 140 years before the Nazis demonstrated that they could commit greater atrocities and exterminate many more people than the revolutionary Committee of Public Safety. The comparison, however, is unfair in that the Nazis had gas chambers and other modern techniques of mass extermination at their disposal. The French only had the guillotine and grapeshot, which in a way was fortunate because the extent of the genocide they may have effected, armed as the Germans were, would probably have decimated the population. Nethertheless, until the advent of the Third Reich the French revolutionary government probably held the dubious European record for a government policy based on injustice and sheer bloody murder. So much then for the long French intellectual debates on the subject of human rights, the groundwork of which, in England, had been laid down fairly bloodlessly almost 500 years previously at Runnymede.

Finally, the execution of Louis XVl did nothing to stabilise the country. Had it been possible to form a viable constitutional monarchy, which in all fairness was the original intent at that time, it might have brought continuity and with it a stabilising effect, avoiding the schism between Republicans and Royalists.

'In a civil war a general must know ... when to move over to the other side?'
Henry Reed: *Not a Drum was Heard*

The schism still exists, and recognition of this helped me to understand the phenomenon of the Vichy government during the Second World War. A large proportion of French people supported this government and they probably did so because the values of 'Work, Family and Homeland', as proclaimed by Vichy, were much nearer to their beliefs than the values of 'Liberty, Equality and Fraternity', proclaimed by the Republic. The supporters of fascist Vichy, whether in the so-called 'free zone' or in occupied France, did not see themselves as collaborators with the Germans but rather as their partners in building a new Europe, and as such quite expected to inherit any fragments of the British Empire that the Germans deigned to give them once the war was ended with a German victory. Unfortunately for Vichy, the Nazis did not see things in quite the same light. They regarded France generally as a decadent country and would much have preferred to arrive at some sort of peace agreement with Britain. Perhaps the greatest humiliation for the grubby little men of Vichy and their supporters lay in their unawareness that, despite their strenuous efforts to please, the Germans did not want them as allies. Be that as it may, no other occupied country in Europe has such a dismal wartime record as France. The Lavals of the 1940s slipped easily into the shoes of the Robespierres of the 1790s and orchestrated a second reign of terror. No other occupied country carried out a persecution of the Jews by its own forces of law and order to the extremes carried out in France, even to the extent of being well in excess of the German demands. However, one cannot compare the position of the French under Vichy to that of the populace in other occupied countries. The Vichy government was not imposed by Germany; it was a French government, seeking independence through co-operation. Given that it had the support of a significant proportion of the people, there was little that the average non-politically minded citizen could do but accept it.

The Vichy government, however, did not represent the whole French nation. Many French men and women fled to fight bravely with De Gaulle, and many who remained risked their own lives to save the lives of Jews and to resist the occupation. Those who remained echoed the cry that has reverberated throughout France for centuries whenever a national crisis occurs. 'We are betrayed', which of course they were. In fact, so far as the many French communists were concerned, not only were they betrayed but they were also in a dilemma of conflicting loyalties. Nazi Germany had signed a non-aggression pact with that other land of the free, Soviet Russia. Together they were happy busily carving up Poland, so what was a good communist to think and where did his loyalties lie? It was only after the German invasion of Russia in June 1941 that the myriad French communists got their act together and become an effective resistance force. By 1943, when the outcome of the war was no longer in much doubt, becoming associated with the resistance was the wise thing to do and many politicians and fellow travellers suddenly discovered that they were not fascists at all but had always been loyal to the Republic. Even the police, who had been so efficient in carrying out the Nazi doctrine of fear and oppression, picked up their rifles when the Americans were at the gate and the liberation of Paris was imminent, and started shooting at the occupying forces. Probably with shouts of '*Vive la France*' and '*Vive la Republique*'.

Despite earnest attempts by succeeding governments initially to hide, and in later years to come to terms with, the sins of Vichy, and despite the accent on Republican values stressed at the school level, there still remains the same division within France. The ultra-right wing now pulls in some 16 per cent of votes while the communists, although weakening, refuse to change the party name to something more palatable and still hold on to some 10 per cent of the vote. Simple addition would seem to demonstrate that a quarter of the French voters are political extremists.

Thinking about the dismal panoply of French history, I concluded that a thousand years of betrayal, war and civil strife had bred an underlying sense of insecurity into the French psyche and that this inbred insecurity went a long way to explaining why the Frenchman is suspicious, not only of his neighbour, but of life in general. He is always expecting a betrayal in one form or another. Should good fortune happen to come his way, then he is sure that he will have to pay for it sooner or later. There is, he believes, always someone who is about to take him for a *con*. If this person is not an Anglo-Saxon, then it is the next-door neighbour or a close associate. This suspicion, based on fear, results in an unpleasant side to the French character. The Frenchman is capable of informing on his neighbour, an action that the average Britisher would find revolting. However, this unpleasant tendency is nothing new. I have a bank note issued by the Republic in 1791, or, as dated with the classical intellectual arrogance of revolutionaries: the 10th of Brumaire of the year 2. Anyway, regardless of whatever date one chooses to use, the note is an '*Assignat De Cinq Livres*'. Apart from such stirring slogans as: '*Liberté, Egalité et Fraternité ou La Morte*' and '*Unité, Indivisibilité De La République*' printed in the corners, the note also carries the message that '*La Nation Récompense Le Denonciateur*'. That is to say, 'The State will reward informers'. Charming!

The Artful Dodger

Informing on one's neighbour is still not unknown in France, but informing who about what is another story. The Frenchman these days will rarely, if ever, inform the police about anything. In fact, if he believes he has a common enemy, outside of the dreaded Anglo-Saxon, it is the unfortunate police. He will go to pains to alert everyone of the presence of police. The only time he is a considerate road user is when he spots police activity. He will then alert all oncoming traffic for the next couple of miles by frantically flashing his headlights. Neither does he show any tendency to inform local authorities of contraventions against local bylaws. He will leave his neighbour alone to plant as many trees or to build whatever he likes in his garden or to hang his washing out on a Sunday. The Frenchman will, however, happily and anonymously inform the income tax authorities should he suspect his neighbour of having a lifestyle beyond his means. He will also inform should he suspect misuse of the social security services. He does not, apparently, appreciate anybody taking advantage of the state, or perhaps – and to me this is the most likely reason – he wants to ingratiate himself with the authorities as a form of self-preservation.

However, with typical French inconsistency there is one particularly common tax dodge which well illustrates the triumph of the Frenchman's need to prove he can beat the system over his desire to keep on the right side of whatever authority happens to be in power. This dodge takes place at the time of a house sale, should the seller be liable for tax on the sale, as for example in the case of inheritance or capital gains. The rules are as follows: The seller, after the usual negotiations, will agree the selling price on the basis that the purchaser pays a certain sum in cash. The sale is registered at the agreed price less the cash amount. The next step is to contact a solicitor to draw up the purchase contract. Now, of course, there is a slight problem as up to now no money has changed hands and the seller is relying upon the purchaser's word that he will cough up the agreed amount in cash at the moment of signing the final purchase contract. This is an impossible situation because no Frenchman will trust another one. However, *Système D* comes to the rescue and the estate agent may be prepared to draw up two separate agreements, the first at the actual selling price and the second at the lower false selling price, lower because the amount promised in cash has been deducted. All parties arrive at the solicitor's office at the time of the contract signature, whereupon the buyer hands over the cash to the seller before meeting with the solicitor. The solicitor is then presented with the lower purchase price and everything proceeds normally. Everybody is happy and the seller has had the security of having the second price agreement in his pocket should the purchaser have failed to produce the cash.

There is not really much advantage for either party in this game as the amount paid in cash cannot be allowed to make the official purchase price too low, as this may look suspicious. The buyer saves a little on legal fees as they are proportional to the purchase price and the seller may gain a little on any capital gains tax due from the house sale. It seems a great deal of trouble to go to for very little. However, for the Frenchman, the real pleasure is that he has been able to beat the system. Everybody recognises this dodge and there is therefore no need to be secretive about the exact amount one pays for a house. New to a neighbourhood, people are naturally curious about the price you have paid and eventually may ask you, indirectly of course, about the purchase price. If you tell them, they will then ask whether or not the figure you gave them included the amount that was passed 'under the table'.

'Always suspect everybody'
Charles Dickens: *The Old Curiosity Shop*

A current of suspicion permeates most aspects of life in France. In any business arrangement the spoken word has little to no value, which is fair enough maybe in this day and age. However, little value is put upon the simple written word either. To protect themselves in as many ways as humanly possible and to ensure that the risk of being taken for a *con* is minimised, the French go to great lengths with any written agreement. One signature has apparently no significance, and therefore contracts are initialled upon each page with here and there a full signature required prefaced by the words '*Lu et Apprové*', that is to say, 'Read and Agreed'. This process does tend to make the purchase of a house a much more friendly affair than in the UK. Spending the better part of a morning or afternoon in a solicitor's office signing away busily some 40 or more pages, one chats to the solicitor and can eventually come to regard him as an old friend. So much different from the cold half-hour or less that one spends in the UK with only one or two signatures to make on the couple of pages of a single purchase contract.

This twisted belief that all the world is dishonest is again demonstrated in the sending of any important registered letter. Here one is advised not to put the letter in an envelope in the normal way but to fold the paper, glue it and then address it on the obverse side. When I first met with this practice I asked why one earth would anyone want to do that. The answer I received was that if I enclosed the letter in an envelope then the recipient could always claim that he had not received the letter but only an empty envelope. Therefore, I was told, is absolutely customary to send the letter without an envelope. Any questions?

As a subject of Her Gracious Majesty trying to integrate into the culture of the French, I arrived at the conclusion that our different historical backgrounds would be more than sufficient to give us very different perceptions of the world and could easily be responsible for the tendency of the French to be both insecure and suspicious in their daily lives.

'In their religion they are so uneven'
Daniel Defoe: *The True-Born Englishman*

If history has played a role in developing insecurity into French culture and security into the English, there are also the effects of religion and geography to consider. Officially France is now a secular republic, but it seems that it borders on the impossible for any French government to achieve anything simply. The conflict for political power which was waged between the state and the church in Christian Europe from the time of Charlemagne and the creation of the Holy Roman Empire was terminated in England in 1534. Henry VIII used the simple expedient of having himself declared supreme head of the Church of England, ousting the Pope from that position and thus uniting the two forces under one head, but then Henry did have the habit of finding effective, even if somewhat draconian, solutions to most of life's irritations. Things were not so simple in France and it was not until 1905 that legislation was passed separating the church from the state. Naturally, being France, this was a painful procedure, giving ample opportunity for the French to riot and bash each other once again and for armed soldiers with fixed bayonets to harass the clergy.

The major religion practised in France is Roman Catholicism and so both France and Britain share a Christian culture. However, there is at least one significant difference between the spiritual comfort offered by the Roman Catholic faith and that offered by the Protestant, which is the role of the priest in the act of confession. The Catholic has the benefit of confessing to God and seeking forgiveness for his sins through the intermediary of the priest and knowing that a man of God is interceding for him. He can leave the confession reassured that he is forgiven. The Protestant stands on his own before God, without the benefit of an intermediary, and confesses to God alone. He can then only trust that God forgives him his sins but he has no official assurance from a third party that

50

this is the case. Is it any wonder that Luther suffered from constipation?

The Catholic practice of worshipping the Virgin as the mother of God gives the Deity the sense of a family where the child can approach his kind but stern father through appealing to the gentleness of his mother. Protestantism seems to me to be a much harder interpretation of Christianity. In England, however, Protestantism possibly did allow a social climate which facilitated the growth of capitalism. The entrepreneurial spirit probably flourishes easier in a Protestant environment, and the fact that the Industrial Revolution occurred first in England may possibly owe something to the Protestant faith. The belief that man stands alone in the face of God permits an individual to believe that he alone has to justify his actions before God and that he has no need to confess and be sanctioned by a third party. Although this may encourage him to feel a greater responsibility for his actions, it also opens the door to many interpretations of Christian morality. Briefly, in the extreme case, the nineteenth-century capitalist was able to cruelly exploit his workers if he so wished and yet remain able to reconcile such behaviour with Christianity, a sort of Orwellian 'doublethink'. Even in later years it is interesting to note that the policy of apartheid was practised in a Protestant country.

'Food out of the earth and wine that maketh glad the heart of man'
Psalm 104

The Industrial Revolution in England accelerated the population drift from the country to the city and this process, aided by that sense of individual responsibility which was nurtured by the Protestant faith, sowed the seeds of another Protestant first, the gradual break-up of family life. In France the combination of Catholicism with an agricultural life lent support to the concept of the family. In terms of festivities there are many more religious holidays in France than in Britain. Ascen-

51

sion, Assumption and All Saints are all examples. In addition most French children are named after saints and have their 'saint's day' celebrated, perhaps not with the same enthusiasm as a birthday, but celebrated nevertheless. This can mean that in a family of six, including the parents, there are 12 birthdays or saints' days to be celebrated by the family as well as the official religious holidays.

Historical and religious influences apart, there is also the effect of geographical location and climate on a nation's culture. Unlike Britain, surrounded by its protective girdle of sea, France has five land frontiers, which makes it difficult if not impossible to effectively control ingress and egress. It is only possible to attempt to control immigration through internal controls, and the identity card serves this purpose. Whereas the British can wander freely around their country carrying no identification at all, the Frenchman risks at any time being asked by a policeman to produce his identification card. Failure to produce it does not entail any penalty whatsoever but could, depending upon circumstance, lead to the tedious business of accompanying the policeman to the station and waiting there while enquiries are made to prove that you are who you say you are. This is only true in theory, because after 26 years in France I have never yet been asked to produce mine; maybe I look honest.

France is a country where nature has been generous. It is bounded by the warm Mediterranean to the south and the Atlantic to the west, giving it a variable climate and enabling it to produce a range of fruit, vegetables, dairy products and, most importantly, wine. Britain, on the other hand, surrounded by cold seas suffers a wetter, colder climate. The quantity and variety of food and wine available to the French *paysan* must have played a significant role in focusing his attention on food as a pleasure to be enjoyed and not, as for many English, a necessity to be consumed as rapidly as possible so as not to waste time. Visits to various friends made me aware of the fact that in traditional French houses either the kitchen or the dining room is the focal point for social activities. Unlike the English, who tend to furnish their houses with the lounge or sitting room as the social centre, the French concentrate on the table as their centre-piece. Lounges are rarely in evidence. Invited to a Frenchman's house, one is almost invariably sat at the table, and even should the invitation exclude a meal, a bottle of wine is soon forthcoming. It was further proof for me of the importance of food and wine to the French culture.

The French worker is entitled to purchase his jug of wine during his lunch break in the factory canteen, a practice which startled and even alarmed many of the American managers who visited the factories in which I was working. The willingness to open a bottle of champagne at the least pretext was also evident in the working environment. Unfortunately the advent of the desk computer has dramatically changed the industrial lifestyle, but in the 1970s and 1980s it was the habit to throw a works party at the slightest occasion. Word would be passed around that it was somebody's birthday or promotion or whatever, and people would congregate in that person's workplace, usually at the end of the day or during the lunch break, to celebrate the occasion with bottles of champagne.

In France as in Britain, holidays, birthdays and even saints' days are all opportunities for a celebration, but in France they are frequently spent with the family, around the table, often outdoors, enjoying fresh food and wine. This is an entirely different affair from my memories of a 1960s Sunday tea with my then mother-in-law. We laboured through a menu of corned beef and daintily cut cucumber sandwiches, followed by canned peaches with evaporated milk and terminated the event with a cup of tea, while during the whole of the late afternoon the rain ran down the windowpanes. I wondered whether, if the French had the same diet as the British, they would be so ready to celebrate on every occasion around the table. Alternatively, if the French were of the Protestant faith, would they find other reasons to celebrate so frequently with food and wine surrounded by their families?

Putting together the influences of history, religion and climate on French culture and comparing how these same influences had impacted upon the way I, with my British culture, understood the world, I felt that I could perhaps begin to perceive the world through French eyes. In my mind the Frenchman emerged as a person deeply suspicious of his neighbour and of all authority, retaining above all a deeply ingrained dislike of all things Anglo-Saxon. His close domestic ties, strong enough to diminish his needs to find friends outside his family circle, helped to convince him that his standards were the only true standards to live by. He was, justifiably, proud of the produce of his country, and his soul was still planted firmly in the values of the peasant. Outside his close family environment he felt insecure, trusting no one and needing constant reassurance that his intelligence was high enough to protect him from the traps and pitfalls that lay in his path. A complicated people, but I was determined to understand them. If to do that it was necessary to become as French as possible for anyone born and educated in an Anglo-Saxon culture, then I was prepared to make the effort. I wanted the French company for which I worked not only to wish to retain my services, but also to offer me a career development. I liked living in France and I intended to stay there.

5

FELIPE AND JIM

Sometime around 1976, Felipe paid me two backhanded compliments, which I accepted with some pleasure, understanding him well enough by then to realise that these were the only type of compliments that he was prepared to pay anyone. One afternoon he had wandered into my office and made himself comfortable in one of the small armchairs that I kept for visitors. Knowing Felipe, I took this for a signal that he was indulging in one of his 'management by walking around' exercises and wanted to bring himself up to date on the latest events in the engineering department. I poured us each a cup of coffee and spent some minutes outlining the progress on the key projects that we were then engaged in, before bringing the conversation round to some of the changes that I was thinking of making in the department. To be effective, a management structure must be dynamic and responsibilities need to change within the team to meet the evolving competence of each individual member. Developing the high-flyers within an organisation is the easy part of the problem, the real challenge lies in ensuring that the average middle manager is taking on the tasks best suited to his abilities. I talked to Felipe about what I thought would improve the performance of one or two of the less brilliant managers who were proving difficult to integrate into the team. Felipe could never become very interested in low performers and, finishing his coffee, he rose from his chair to signify that our little break was over and that it was time for us to get back to work. Pausing at the office door before he left he turned towards me and said:

'I would always give you a job because you can do the one thing that I find impossible.'

'What is that?' I asked, somewhat flattered.

'Work with idiots,' he replied.

As was so often the case with Felipe, there was no answer to that. In fact Felipe was a very humane man with a high degree of empathy and understanding, but he had a low threshold of tolerance for anything or any person that he considered unintelligent, and he set a fairly high standard. If one had put aside all the people that Felipe considered idiots, it would have significantly reduced the company's management team.

A few months later he told me that I was useful because I could manage the intangibles. I was not sure exactly what he meant by this comment but it cheered me considerably. I felt that the time and effort I had put into trying to understand the French had not been just an exercise in intellectual masturbation on my part but was really helping me to accept and be accepted by my colleagues. In fact I began to suspect that I could understand the French mentality as well if not even better than he, Latin though he may have been. Not bad, I thought, for a dreaded Anglo-Saxon.

I was to lose Felipe as a boss a little later, but not before I had developed an enormous degree of respect for him, while for his part I believe that he found me a useful member of his team. He was promoted and transferred to the company's operation in Spain and replaced in France by a Canadian, Jim Boyd. So far as I was concerned, my department was healthy and gaining in importance, while the company continued to expand and make a steady profit. Everything was rosy, and although I would miss the pleasure of working with Felipe, I settled down to work for Jim Boyd. He, unfortunately, was not to enjoy his time in France. He was a slow and careful thinker, ill matched for the explosive and erratic contortions of French management. His staff meetings bordered on the chaotic. Jim would embark on a lengthy monologue, silencing any attempt at an interruption while he slowly enumerated his ideas of the logical approach to a particular project. He would advance his ideas step by painful step, while the French managers fidgeted in their seats. They anxiously awaited the first opportunity to interrupt him so that they could discuss the many associated problems which they had identified before Jim had finished his first sentence. His approach infuriated the French and they would writhe in agony until one of them could contain himself no longer and would burst into Jim's monologue with a cry of '*Mais non*! *Mais non*! *Il y a un problème*'. This was usually the signal for the meeting to descend into chaotic disorder.

Citizen Cockroach

Jim's wife Margaret, a most charming woman, was also unhappy in France, despite living in a very handsome apartment in one of the better areas to the west of Paris. She told me that, amongst other things, she missed the range of instant food readily available in North America but still at that time in its infancy in France. The sparsity of convenience foods in the shops appeared to be one of her concerns, but given that its superfluity in England was one of the reasons why I was in France, I had difficulty in relating to her on this matter. However, without any doubt at all the major problem which confronted her and obviously gave her nightmares was that she had to contend with that ubiquitous Parisian denizen, the cockroach. Margaret could not accept the presence of cockroaches in any area and certainly not in the rather upmarket arrondissement where Jim and she had chosen to live. They filled her with horror.

Infestation in an apartment of such standing is, however, fairly readily explainable. The French architects of the period, determined to equip their apartments with all mod cons, had installed a rubbish chute in each kitchen – a simple device allowing the cook to dispose of household rubbish through a flap set in the kitchen wall. The rubbish then fell down a tube into a large container in the basement from where it was regularly collected and disposed of. There is absolutely no reason why these rubbish chutes should not have been both effective and hygienic, if only the users had taken the pains to wrap their rubbish, and specifically their moist rubbish, in plastic bags before disposal. Unfortunately, the French architects failed to understand the habits of the French cook. Given easy disposal of rubbish, the Frenchman or woman will, with a nonchalant gesture and a merry heigh-ho, tend to sling everything down the chute. The result is that in a very short time the inside of the rubbish chute becomes encrusted with all sorts of gunge, from coffee grounds to leftovers from yesterday's *pot-au-feu. Bonjour*, Citizen Cockroach: who will have no hesitation whatsoever in inviting all his family, friends and relations to join him in a beano and rapidly infest every kitchen in the block.

The cockroach translated into French is *le cafard*, but it is also a word which can be incorporated into a phrase to give other meanings. '*Avoir le cafard*' translates into English as 'feeling blue' while '*ça me donne le cafard*' can be translated as 'it makes me homesick'. Poor Margaret Boyd had *cafards* in every sense of the word and just lived for the day when she could return with her husband to the hygienic snows of Canada.

Although by 1976 everything was going well so far as my career was concerned, the same could not be said for my domestic life. My two children returned to the UK to live their own lives and my wife decided that she too wished to return home, giving as her reason the need to take care of her aged father, who was a widower. However, by this time not only was I committed to a French career but I also preferred living in France and had no desire to exchange it for the uncertainties of life in Jim Callaghan's inflation-ridden economy. A family break-up was inevitable and finally led to a relatively amicable separation and divorce.

After my wife and children had returned to England, I continued living on my own in the house in Neuilly-sur-Marne. I am fairly self-sufficient in terms of looking after myself and actually quite enjoy cooking and messing about generally in the kitchen, with the accent probably more on messing about than on *haute cuisine*. However, to my mind cooking every evening, especially if it is just for oneself, becomes rather a bore after a while, and I began to fully understand how the average wife must feel faced with the monotony of preparing meals for a family at the rate of two or even three a day. Once in a while it was pleasant preparing a dinner for invited friends at the weekend, but spending an hour or so in the kitchen every evening was a bit much.

Partially to avoid the chore of cooking and partially because of loneliness, I fell into the habit of working long into the evening then driving to the Left Bank and having my evening meal in one of the numerous small restaurants that crowd that area. I would enjoy my late meal, linger over a coffee and a cognac and then stroll along the banks of the Seine, soaking in the atmosphere and watching the boats crowded with tourists illuminating Notre Dame and the buildings on the Ile St Louis. Finally tired, I would then drive back to Neuilly around midnight and go straight to bed.

It was a lonely life and a celibate one, and I felt that after all I was in Paris and should at least have some feminine company. I had long believed that to really enter into the spirit of Paris and enjoy life there, it is necessary either to be young and in love or else to be rich and any age. I was neither. However, looking on the bright side, I was earning good money and was not yet in my dotage. There had to be a solution. A working colleague, Igor, who was nearer to 50 than I was and living alone in his Paris apartment, had his own way of handling the problem, at least so far as finding women was concerned. Igor, originally from Estonia, had emigrated to England sometime during the very early days of the war and was a specialist in the hygiene standards required in the confectionery industry. He had been working for the same company as I in the UK and was in France on a temporary assignment, bringing his expertise to advise on those hygiene measures that needed to be incorporated into the French expansion programme. His sexual appetite was insatiable and he had tried to get every woman in the factory into bed without any success. This was hardly surprising as his seduction techniques were, to say the least, basic, resembling if anything those of a fairly polite but very oversexed bull let loose in a field of cows. Consequently all the girls in the factory and offices had learned to keep at least 4 feet away from him whenever his job brought him into their presence. Igor had finally solved his problem by answering a weird advert in a rather disreputable Parisian weekly that offered to supply one with an introductory list of exciting girls for a reasonable down payment, after which you were on your own. Igor was enthralled and seemed to have found his sexual paradise, but it was not to last. I met him one day in the factory yard and told him that he really did look pale and worn out and that he should not overdo things at work but perhaps take a day off to rest. Work, he told me, was not the problem. He had now reached number six on his exciting girl list. Number six had turned out to be a rather large coloured American girl whose sexual appetite even surpassed that of Igor, and to complicate the matter the girl had taken quite a fancy to him, so much so in fact that he could not now get rid of her.

'I can't keep it up,' he informed me.

'Keep off the vodka,' I advised him.

'I mean I can't keep up the pace, you clot. It's killing me,' he said. 'She's been coming around every evening and I'm frightened that she intends to move in with me.'

Actually it was more difficult to avoid sex in Paris than to find it. These were the days before AIDS had been heard of and prostitution in all its forms, both male and female, was very much alive and well throughout the city, while an evening drive through the Bois de Boulogne or the Bois de Vincennes was made hazardous by the lines of kerb-crawlers and the sudden visions of naked breasts and thighs caught in the glare of one's headlights. This readily available sex was of no interest to me. I was not in that market. I was looking for a respectable girlfriend who would be a companion not just a sexual partner, and finding such a person was not proving to be such an easy matter. I had been a relatively faithful husband for nearly 20 years and was more than a little rusty on the gentle art of seduction. To complicate matters, French girls, I discovered, were not susceptible to the same approach that I had used with some success on English girls in my distant past. They were coy and far more adept at the finer points of courtship than those I had been used to practise on the top deck of a late-night Liverpool tram. They enjoyed the flirtation and the teasing surrounding sexual approaches and I never knew exactly where I stood with them. They tantalised me. Unlike most of the English girls I had known, the French girl seemed to enjoy her feminity and expected to be admired and courted. She knew how to accept compliments and revelled in them, a far cry from the 'Ooooh! Don't be daft' response of the Liverpool girl of my youth when told that her eyes were like limpid forest pools. Whatever, I made several attempts to cultivate a girlfriend without much success, but it was probably my relatively clumsy overtures that resulted in each dismal failure. Then I found Jocelyne, or at least she found me.

Jocelyne collected admirers. A bachelor girl living alone in a small apartment on a corner between the rue Mouffetard and l'Estrapade Contrescarp, she was obviously determined to enjoy her young life and the company of men friends. I had met her one Saturday morning while browsing around a bookshop on the rue de Rivoli. I had taken to the habit of driving into Paris early on a Saturday when it was still possible to find a parking place and, leaving the car, stroll up the avenue de l'Opéra. I would spoil myself with breakfast in the Café de la Paix and later walk down the rue de la Paix to its end on the rue de Rivoli. There I would call into one or two bookshops on the way back to my parked car.

Jocelyne, although she didn't know it at the time, was looking for an English language copy of Orwell's *The Road to Wigan Pier*, but she was having a little difficulty in remembering the exact title of the book. Overhearing her discussion of the theme of the book with the salesgirl and having read all of Orwell's works, I thought that I could be of assistance, and anyway I was always ready to try and help a pretty girl in distress. I hastened to offer my aid and suggested the title Jocelyne was looking for. She thanked me, and once she had ordered her book we left the bookshop together and it seemed natural that I should then offer her a coffee at the nearest

61

pavement café. She accepted, and we sat in the sun discussing Orwell while we sipped our expressos and watched the morning traffic begin to build up around the Jardin des Tuileries. It seemed that we both had an interest in Orwell as a writer, and from a discussion of his work our conversation turned to other authors and then to paintings and the latest exhibition at the Grand Palace and so on. It was all very intellectual and ended with me inviting her to have a meal with me one evening whenever she was free. She agreed and we finally made a date for the following Friday evening.

We met at a cosy little Chinese restaurant on the Left Bank. Comfortably installed at a table for two, we ordered the house aperitif and perused the menu while sipping the rose-flavoured drink. Jocelyne enjoyed Chinese food and I was hungry, so we studied the menu with some anticipation. Over *Crevettes à la sauce aigre douce* we discussed literature and later, mellowed by a bottle of Tavel, reviewed our philosophies of life while savouring sweet Chinese almond cakes. We idled over our coffee until the waiter offered each of us a tiny cup of rice liqueur, and after we had drunk that I offered to drive Jocelyne home.

Parking the car in Contrescarpe was an impossibility but I eventually found a space near to Le Panthéon and walked Jocelyne the remaining few hundred yards to her apartment building. Hesitating at the door, I turned to leave her, wondering if I could try a goodnight kiss – I was still 20 years behind the times so far as romance was concerned – when she invited me in for a little *digestif* and together we climbed the wooden stairway to the top floor.

Her apartment turned out to be little more than a studio consisting of one main room, the centrepiece of which was a large bed. Against the window was a small table, which apart from some bookshelves and a couple of chairs, completed the furnishing. On either side of the room there was a door, one leading into a small bathroom and the other into an even smaller kitchen. Jocelyne switched on the bedside lamp and I sat at the table while she produced a bottle of cognac and a couple of glasses. We drank looking out of the window at the activitiy in the street below us. It was nearing midnight but the area was still crowded and the restaurants overflowing into the street. In the centre of the crowds a *cracheur de feu* was amusing the customers of the pavement cafés by exhaling yard long sheets of flame into the air, while in the lights from the same cafés a juggler was happily performing with three or four Indian clubs. The atmosphere was that of excited good humour created by a late night crowd enjoying life, an atmosphere which the French would refer to as *'bon enfant'*. We sat together enjoying the scene. It was becoming very late and I told Jocelyne that it was probably time that I made a move to go home. We finished our drinks and she moved away from the table. I turned to look at her. She was standing with her back against the wall, her glass empty in her hand. She was slightly above the average height for a French girl, dark-haired, with an attractive oval face and the greenest eyes I had ever seen. We looked at each other for a second or two and then she gave me a slight smile. 'It's nearly one o clock,' she said. 'Would you like to stay the night with me?'

Surprised but excited, I nodded my head and then turned it away from her as she casually began to undress. Risking a look after a moment, I saw that she stood in her underclothes and she smiled again saying, 'Now I must go to the bathroom.' She walked slowly to the bathroom door, giving me time to appreciate all the lines of her body. She had small breasts, supported, I remember, by a dark green brassiere. Her slim waist accentuated her wide hips and her pronounced buttocks. I waited until she came out of the bathroom and then, taking her place at the washbasin, I undressed and hurridly washed. Coming back into the bedroom, I found Jocelyne in bed with the covers pulled up over her nose and only her green eyes peering at me over the top of the duvet, with her black hair lying tousled on the pillow. I gently eased myself into the bed beside her and felt the long forgotten delight of having a warm, silky, girl's body folded in my arms. We made love more times that night than I thought lay within my capabilities. In the early morning I awakened to feel Jocelyne's body pressed against mine. Gently I let my hand fondle her breasts and then wander down to caress her thighs. She opened her eyes. 'What a lovely way to be awakened,' she sighed sleepily. It was one of the most sexually arousing remarks I had ever heard. We made love again.

Later she made our morning coffee and I gazed from her window on to the rooftops of Paris. This, I thought, is the sort of thing I used to read about but never thought that I would experience. For a few brief minutes I felt a student again, full of confidence and far from business or any other worries. I left, arranging to meet her on the following Friday, and walked out into the morning Paris air feeling at least ten years younger.

My affair with Jocelyne lasted several months, and as I look back they were perhaps amongst the happiest days of my life. I was having a passionate affair with a young and attractive girl in a city which breathed romance. Saturdays we would spend hours together looking through the bookstalls that line the embankments of the Seine, eat our lunch in intimate restaurants on the Left Bank and then visit the museums and art galleries. We would finish our day buying the groceries for our evening meal, cooking them in her tiny kitchen and eating them to the sound of the Contrescarpe crowds enjoying themselves. The nights were spent with passion, making love across the width of her large double bed. I felt that I was falling deeply in love with her but it became evident that while I was searching for a more permanent relationship, she was not. She was enjoying her bachelor life and the easy sex which had arrived in France somewhat later than had been the case in England. Jocelyne enjoyed our lovemaking and the times we spent together but she was not going to be tied down to a steady boyfriend. At least not yet. However, I remained grateful to her, for not only had I experienced a passionate love affair but she also enabled me to overcome my feelings of inadequacy regarding Frenchwomen.

Towards the end of our affair, Jocelyne was to play a role in earning me an unmerited reputation as a Lothario in one of my favourite restaurants. I had discovered a delightful Left Bank restaurant with a tiny privet-hedged terrace looking

64

across the Quai De Montebello directly on to Notre Dame. It was reasonably priced and I used it from time to time in the evenings when I wanted to feel really Parisian. One week in the summer of 1976 a consultant friend of mine who was going away for a week or two asked me if I would mind taking his wife out to a restaurant one evening while he was away as she would be on her own during his absence. Always willing to oblige a friend, and in this case the attractiveness of his wife made the task a pleasure, I assured him that I would. I took her to my little restaurant. The head waiter was obliging and we had a very pleasant meal. It was July and Notre Dame was alight with a *son et lumière* and the view from the restaurant's terrace was superb. We both admired it. A couple of days later it was my secretary's twenty-first birthday and I thought it would be a nice gesture if I asked her to dinner. I had been so impressed by the splendour of the illumination of Notre Dame that I had no hesitation in returning there. The head waiter was even more obliging and I thought I felt a certain amount of respect in the way he took our order, made sure that the wine was served at the right temperature and generally treated me with some deference. That Friday I had my usual date with Jocelyne and decided that it would be romantic if we were to gaze at each other with the huge illuminated rose window of Notre Dame reflected in her eyes. This time the head waiter looked at me with respect mingled with amazement and I realised that Jocelyne was the third attractive woman I had taken to that restaurant in the space of a week. As it grew later and I touched Jocelyne's hand across the table the head waiter became very friendly and when catching my eye would smile and wink at me. A little later I noticed that he had brought the chef out of the kitchen and that both of them were looking at me through the restaurant window, smiling and nodding their heads with definite gestures of admiration.

That meal was one of the last that I shared with Jocelyne. A short time later I was to meet other girls and my romance with Jocelyne faded. We saw less and less of each other until at last we lost contact. Years later we were to meet again but in an entirely different context. It's a small world.

With Jocelyne and other girls, I was to discover that despite their coyness French girls are interested in sex and for the most part enjoy it. Their seduction, however, required slightly different skills from the ones that I had been used to.

In general I found the French attitude to sex to be very different from the English. The taking of a mistress, for example, while not perhaps openly condoned is certainly not frowned upon to the extent that it is in Britain or the States. It is inconceivable in France that a politician or any public figure should lose his reputation and maybe his position through a sex scandal. That President Mitterrand openly acknowledged that he had fathered an illegitimate daughter by one of his mistresses raised no French eyebrow. The fact that he had a mistress was considered more or less normal and the French would probably have been more concerned if he had not had one. Then their reaction would have been 'What's the matter with him?' Reports of politicians losing their posts in the UK because of sexual waywardness are met with complete incomprehension by the French. The importance given to the sexual scandal associated with President Clinton is beyond the understanding of the French; they shrug their shoulders and regard the whole ballyhoo as just another example of Anglo-Saxon weirdness.

Living in France, it is difficult to avoid the subject of sex in daily life. It is used extensively in advertising and it occupies a great deal of television time, either in the form of serious discussion on subjects such as prostitution, homosexuality and other deviations or in the numerous soft-porn movies. The interest of the French in sex is clearly demonstrated in their humour, the majority of their jokes having some sort of sexual connotation. I think that a nation's humour is in fact quite revealing as to certain aspects of its culture. A close look at the humour expressed in international newspapers and periodicals will show that whereas the French laugh at sex, the English laugh at themselves and their institutions. The Spanish find humour in death while German humour tends to be scatological. All very interesting and I am sure that a psychologist could make something out of that.

Unfairly, the Frenchwoman still remains virtually a third-class citizen within the context of a number of French laws, usually those which have their origins in the Napoleonic Code. Napoleon may have been a brilliant military strategist but when it came to women he tended to be misogynous. One of the most striking examples of unfairness to women lies in the French laws of inheritance. When considering making a will, I was told by my French solicitor to forget it as I would only complicate matters. Under French law one cannot disinherit one's children and they automatically inherit between 50 per cent and 75 per cent of one's estate, depending upon their number, a situation that can put a widow's financial future completely in the hands of her children. Even in the event of a childless marriage, surviving parents take precedence over a wife when it comes to inheritance. Apparently when the great intellects defined the rights of men they overlooked to some degree the rights of women. Certainly there are ways in which a wife can be protected, either through holding insurance policies naming her as beneficiary or by the type of matrimonial contract established at the time of the marriage. Basically, however, these are devices to escape an unjust law which penalises the woman who has perhaps spent 40 years or more of her life supporting her husband through the good and bad times. Should her husband die before her, then under French law the wife has virtually no rights of inheritance from her husband's estate, while her children or grandchildren or even parents-in-law do have such rights. It's a man's world.

Introducing My French Family
After the Manner of Women (Genesis 2:1)

Eventually I was to meet and fall in love with a fellow divorcee in the person of a young Frenchwoman, Annie, who would become my second wife. The knowledge that I was to marry into a French family brought with it the realisation that France was to become my home and that I would probably spend the rest of my life there. I relinquished my expatriate status and took a French contract with my employer, accepting that this made a return to the UK virtually out of the question so far as the company was concerned. Annie and I rented a small apartment in Vincennes and I gave the legally required three months' notice to quit the house that I was still renting in Neuilly-sur-Marne. Our intention was that I would move in with Annie in due course, but for three months I passed my time between the two places. Life settled down to a degree of normality and I was then immersed in a completely French environment both at home and at work.

Annie, her daughter Christelle from her previous marriage and I celebrated our first Christmas together as a family in 1978 at the home of my future mother-in-law. I later vowed that this would be the last Christmas I would spend in the French tradition. We arrived at the house around 7 p.m. on Christmas Eve, there to meet numerous aunts and uncles and their children. The evening began with an aperitif, which we took while circulating among the guests and going through the kissing and handshaking procedures which take place whenever French families and friends meet each other. Then we sat at the table and, with the exception of an occasional break, we remained there until 6 a.m. on Christmas morning. The main breaks in this digestive marathon consisted of a visit to the local church to celebrate midnight mass and the arrival of Father Christmas around 1 a.m. For this latter event the children were brought down from their beds to open their presents amid accompanying oohs! and aahs! from the adult audience. The main activity, however, was centred around appreciating the various delicious dishes and wines which came in an unending procession from the kitchen. From time to time there would be a pause for a *Trou normand* in the form of a well-chilled calvados, supposedly a great aid to the digestive juices. On such occasions the hardier members of the family would take time out for a dance around the small space left free in the dining room, before returning to the table for the next course.

Annie and I finally arrived back in Vincennes at 8 a.m. on Christmas morning and spent the rest of Christmas Day asleep in bed. Since then we have always celebrated Christmas English style, with a Christmas Day lunch at the respectable hour of 2 p.m. This is enjoyed by the family, although mother-in-law, who always joins us, claims that she is unable to detect the taste difference between Christmas pudding and mince pies. I have to admit that she has a point.

The Bold Gendarmes

Annie's Vincennes apartment was reasonably cockroach-free. We had sealed off the rubbish chute. Although this minimised the infestation problem, it did create a certain complexity for Annie in terms of rubbish disposal as her apartment was on the third floor. I solved this by suggesting that I would collect her domestic rubbish during my frequent visits and place it with my own rubbish in the dustbin at the Neuilly house. This dustbin was emptied by the local council every two days, which incidentally is typical in the Parisian area. The system worked well. I was running a second-hand Citroën DS in those days, a vehicle equipped with a very large boot and able to contain, if necessary, all the rubbish that Annie was liable to generate in a week. While this had the advantage of making the vehicle an excellent dustcart it did unfortunately result in me tending to forget about the rubbish from time to time. As I had other things than refuse disposal on my mind and no other cause to use the boot, significant amounts of rubbish would sometimes accumulate there until a rather offensive smell would remind me that I had forgotten to get rid of it.

About this time a well-known Baron had disappeared, the victim apparently of a kidnap, and all Paris was abuzz with the news. 'Where is the Baron?' ran the headlines in the national tabloids, and the entire Paris police force were setting up roadblocks and searching every nook and cranny trying to find his whereabouts, but all to no avail.

It happened that one evening I was invited to a party thrown by one of the secretaries, Francesca, a charming girl of Italian extraction who lived in a large house in Le Raincy, a pleasant suburb some few kilometres from the factory. The party became rather wild, with champagne corks popping in all directions, and by the early hours of the morning it was evident that I was in no condition to drive the Citroën or any other car anywhere. Francesca and her husband were concerned about me attempting to drive home and, having a guest bedroom, kindly suggested that I stay overnight with them. I was happy to accept the invitation.

The following morning, feeling more than a little rough, I swallowed a quick cup of coffee and Francesca and I left for work. I took the wheel of the Citroën and, following Francesca in her 2 CV, headed towards the factory. Within 100 yards my car collected a puncture in the rear nearside wheel and, cursing, I pulled into the kerb and stopped it. The spare wheel of the Citroën DS is located beneath the bonnet in front of the engine, so still cursing and with an aching head, I opened the bonnet, took out the spare and changed the wheel. Francesca, who had also stopped, left her 2 CV and stood on the pavement patiently waiting for me to complete the job. I hurriedly tightened the wheel nuts, threw the punctured tyre in the space under the bonnet left vacant by the spare wheel and, once back in the car, accelerated away from the kerb, with my head now throbbing even more than it had previously.

In a little while I became aware through the pain hammering behind my eyes that it seemed to be getting darker and that my vision was becoming somewhat impaired. In fact, after changing the wheel I had not closed the bonnet correctly and it was slowly rising in front of me like the bow of a ship caught in a heavy swell. It continued its ascent until it finally hit the windscreen, whereupon it immediately shattered it. I stopped the car once more and got out of it. I tried to close the bonnet but the impact had distorted it and as a result it refused to close completely. We were only about 2 miles from the factory and I discovered that if I crouched behind the steering wheel in a half standing position I could just peer through the shattered windscreen over the top of the bonnet, although it

70

did flop about a bit and threaten to rise like the phoenix if I exceeded 15 miles per hour. In this way I started off again and continued to follow Francesca, who had evidently decided that she would not forsake me during this stressful moment of my life.

We would probably have arrived at the factory without further incident if there had not been a police block a little further down the road. A very impressive-looking gendarme signalled me to stop and then approached the driver's side of the car. He saluted politely and, completely ignoring my unusual driving position and the crumpled bonnet of the car, said:

'*Vos papiers*, monsieur.'

Satisfied after examining my papers that they were in order, he stood back and regarded the car.

'*Ouvrez le coffre, s'il vous plâit,*' was his next request.

'There is nothing in the boot,' I replied.

The gendarme was not satisfied with this reply and, certainly suspecting that he was about to attain fame by finding the missing Baron in the boot of my Citroën, repeated his request in a much sterner voice.

'*Ouvrez le coffre, monsieur.*'

Reluctantly I followed the gendarme round to the rear of the car and, unsuccessfully trying to say in French 'You're not going to believe this', I gently opened the boot. Together we stared at the collection of fish heads, paper bags, empty cans and other kitchen debris which had been swirling around the boot for the last couple of days.

I have a lot of respect for that gendarme. He was imperturbable. He didn't say a word. He just looked at me and I looked back at him. Eventually I shrugged my shoulders and he shrugged his in return. Francesca, who had stopped her 2 CV about 50 yards ahead of us and walked back to join us, was creased with laughter. '*Ça va, ça va. C'est un anglais,*' she said.

The gendarme regarded me with a look of dawning comprehension on his face as if the realisation that I was English was sufficient to explain the shattered windscreen, the crumpled bonnet, the contents of the car boot and my unorthodox driving position. Everything, in fact.

'*Bien, monsieur, continuez,*' he said.

I returned to my stance behind the steering wheel and drove off.

A month or so later, accompanied in the car by Annie, I had another encounter with the police. Unintentionally I was driving the wrong way up a one-way street, and unfortunately at the same time a police van was proceeding down the same street in the right direction. We came to a halt facing each other and my car was immediately surrounded by about six policemen. Patiently I listened to the tirade addressed to me by the senior officer and meekly handed over all the papers he demanded to see. When finally I could get a word in edgeways I admitted my complete guilt in the affair. To my mind there was nothing else I could do. I told the officer that I was undoubtedly a fool, and a blind one at that, as I really had not seen the one-way street sign. I had no defence whatsoever and could only say that I was sorry. The policeman then asked Annie for her papers which she refused to give him, objecting to his demand on the basis that as she was only a passenger in the car the whole thing had nothing to do with her. The policeman's hackles rose immediately and the situation soon became unpleasant, with both Annie and the policeman becoming more and more heated. Annie's voice became shriller and the policeman's louder. He seemed to have forgotten about me and to be more interested in seeing Annie's driving licence, which she steadfastly refused to show him.

I do not know how the affair would have ended if I had not spoken loudly and sharply in English to Annie. 'For God's sake,' I yelled. 'Show the bloody man your bloody driving licence.' With a murderous look at me, Annie thrust the document under the policeman's nose, and he became pacified immediately. He instructed me to pay more attention to road signs in future, and then the other police held up all the traffic to allow me to turn the car around in the street so that it was facing in the correct direction before we all proceeded on our way. I really believe that my immediate acceptance that I was completely in the wrong, which is something that a Frenchman would never do, so amazed the policeman that he was prepared to let the matter drop and just deliver a caution.

These two occasions have not been my only contact with the forces of law and order in France but, contrary to the Frenchman's concept of the police, I have always found them reasonable.

Felipe Returns

In 1980 I was relocated to the company's main office to the west of Paris and Annie and I then purchased an apartment in a village to the south-west. This was to be the last time in my working life that I would live relatively close to work. Life was as calm and as peaceful as it could be with a French wife and a French stepdaughter of some seven years of age. Then one evening at the beginning of 1981 I received a telephone call. It was Felipe. He was back in Paris, having left the Spanish sister company to take up a directorship in a French soft drink company. I was pleased to speak to him again as it had been nearly five years since I had last had contact with him, although we had exchanged the usual polite greetings each Christmas. We discussed life in general, until he ended the conversation with an invitation for me to have dinner with him one evening the following week.

I hung up the phone, and in answer to Annie's request told her that it was Felipe who had called and that he was back in France.

'Why did he phone you?' she asked.

'Just to say hello and to let me know he was back in France, I suppose. It was just a friendly call,' I replied.

'He didn't phone you for nothing,' said Annie.

'No,' I replied. 'He invited me for dinner.'

'Why?' asked Annie, with typical French suspicion.

'I don't know. He's back in Paris, so I suppose he is just

renewing old contacts. After all, we did get on very well together.'

'Humph,' said Annie. 'There's more to it than that.'

She was right.

Over dinner with Felipe the following week, he offered me the post of manager for the company's largest soft drink bottling factory, which was situated well to the north of Paris and had only recently been acquired by his firm. It lay some 30 miles from the apartment Annie and I had recently purchased. I was hesitant. I fitted well in my present company, the salary was good, I was secure and approaching 50. Felipe, however, was special. He had a brilliant brain and a character that combined humanity with just a slight touch of ruthlessness; above all, his charisma made it impossible to be indifferent to him. The opportunity to work with him again was finally sufficient to persuade me to overcome any reluctance I felt and to accept his offer.

Later, on the way home from the dinner, I wondered what exactly I had let myself in for by accepting to take the reponsibility for 300-odd French workers in a bottling plant situated in a strongly communist area on the other side of Paris to where I was living. I knew nothing about filling bottles. Any experience of bottles that I had to date had been gained in emptying them.

Making Pop

In the early 1980s the soft drink business in France was at the beginning of a huge expansion curve. The French in general did not consume a great deal of the product. Neither did they indulge in snacks. The fast-food burger business had hardly begun. By the 1990s all this was to change, and in the wake of intensive advertising the French were to take to American colas and hamburgers with an alacrity that put many of the small restaurants out of business and generally degraded the quality of the average French cuisine. This change, however, still lay in the future on the day that Felipe introduced me to

74

the factory works committee and I nervously presented myself as their new manager.

The factory had previously been run on very traditional French management lines. That is, in theory *le chef*, which in this case was now me, was all powerful and he made all the decisions. In practice this factory did not run true to form and had over the years established two power centres: the shop steward on one side and the skilled fitters who were responsible for the running of the bottling lines on the other. In practice *le chef* was surplus to requirements.

When Felipe left, I was led into the ex-factory manager's office by the production manager and shown my desk. When I sat down he left me, walking quickly out of the office and shutting the door behind him. I had been in this sort of scenario before and had a feeling of *déjà vu*. Trained in the American 'open door' office policy which had even eventually become the norm at my previous company, I rose from my chair and reopened the door, only to have somebody close it again the moment I had sat down. I stared at the empty desk then once more opened the door. Once more it was closed by the first passer-by, and I began to feel like a character in a Daffy Duck cartoon. I looked around the office and glanced out of the window just in time to notice a small blue van enter the yard and stop by the finished goods warehouse. Moments later a couple of policemen descended and with the help of a labourer began to load the van with crates of soft drinks, then they drove off. I called the warehouse manager, who reassured me that the local police had fairly free access to the warehouse. Incidentally, he added, should I ever have the misfortune to receive a parking ticket, be sure to let him know as he was sure things could be arranged.

I looked again around the office, empty except for my empty desk and my empty self. This, I thought, was another fine mess I'd got myself into. The open the door, shut the door game continued for a couple of days and would probably have continued indefinitely had I not wandered into the small typing pool and asked if any of the girls spoke English.

'I do,' said Yvette.

'Right,' I said. 'Then you can be my secretary if you wish; and if you do, would you please move down into my office.'

She accepted with what I thought to be remarkable alacrity, picked up her typewriter and followed me back to my office. Once she was installed, the first job I gave her was to go out and buy a dozen cups, some ground coffee and a percolator.

The following morning I flung open the office door and bellowed, 'There's coffee going in my office if anyone would like a cup.'

It worked, and although on that first day only three of the fitters and a couple of the office staff made an appearance, by the end of the week the office was packed each morning and we had to send out for more cups. Communication had been established.

The factory had originally been built into and around an existing old building somewhere in the mid-1920s, and any expansion that had taken place in the intervening years had been done, whenever considered necessary by the previous owners, in a haphazard manner with no thought given to potential longer-term needs. It was a maze of conveyers, bottle-washing equipment, filling and labelling machines and all the other sundry items necessary to take an empty return-able bottle, wash it, refill it with a soft drink and prepare it for dispatch to the customer. In terms of hazards to life and limb it was a safety engineer's nightmare. Fork-lift trucks charged in and out of the building like unguided missiles narrowly missing workers and any other pedestrian traffic unfortunate enough to be in the vicinity, while the noise level as some 40,000 bottles per hour crashed through the washing machines was sufficient to deafen everyone in the vicinity. I spent the first few weeks in a state bordering on nervous collapse, expecting at any moment to hear the thud and resultant scream as a fork-lift truck collided with a human body. I would awaken at nights from horrific nightmares of bloody and mangled bodies being hosed down with carbonated water by deaf mutes. I had begun a safety programme on my second day, but time was going to be required before any major improvements could be made. In the meantime the only action I could take was to visit the nearest church and light a candle.

Back Among the Bureaucrats

In these early days I came into contact with two further aspects of French bureaucracy. The first came one mid-morning in the form of a very officious-looking gentleman who represented the Social Security and was concerned with inspecting the working conditions in the factory in terms of safety and hygiene. Feeling apologetic as well as apprehensive as I wondered what the inside of a French prison was like, we made a tour of the factory together, dodging between the hurtling fork-lift trucks that threatened to drastically foreshorten our tour, if not our lives. Any conversation between us being impossible due to the horrendous cacophony emanating from the bottling lines, I thought that the best thing I could do was to invite him to lunch when the tour was finished.

Once sitting in a comfortable restaurant, the official opened the dialogue by stressing his concern about the noise level in the factory. This seemed to concern him more than the murderous trucks, and he read me the riot act on current noise legislation. Then, happily, food was served and it was good. The official was, so he told me, interested in cooking and he took pains to tell me the methods he used in the marination of meat and fish, an activity in which he considered himself to be an undisputed expert. Over an excellent bottle of Bordeaux, he relaxed a little and even seemed pleased when I outlined the safety programme we were developing for the factory and assured him that the company would be most supportive in terms of the investment required. By the end of our lunch, the official and I were on friendly terms and it had been demonstrated to me once more that between reasonable people most problems in France can be resolved around the table. Needless to say, the safety programme was completed and after a few weeks the fork-lift hazard disappeared. It took a little longer to combat the noise level but it was finally achieved.

The second experience was less pleasant and left me with a bit of a nasty taste in the mouth. It was my first, and I hope last, contact with what is perhaps a branch of the French secret police.

Yvette informed me one afternoon as I returned from lunch that she had received a telephone call from a gentleman who wished to see me and that she had arranged for him to meet me in my office the next afternoon.

'Who is he?' I asked.

'He is from les Renseignements Généraux,' she replied.

'Who or what on earth is that? I've never heard of them. It's not somebody else trying to sell me an insurance policy, is it?' I asked her.

'No, nothing like that,' replied Yvette. 'It's a government department, I think. A sort of police force.'

'Then I suppose I'd better see him.'

'Yes,' said Yvette. 'I think you'd better.'

The gentleman whom Yvette ushered into my office the following afternoon shook my hand, introduced himself as Monsieur Martin and smiled ingratiatingly before sitting down.

'I'm from les Renseignements Généraux,' he announced. 'I understand that you are English, so perhaps you would like me to explain what exactly that is.'

'Please do,' I encouraged him. 'Because I have no idea who or what you represent.'

'Well,' he began. 'I'll give you a little historical background first. It all started when the railways were developed in France a long time ago.'

'Yes, that must have been around the mid-nineteenth century,' I interposed. 'Because I think the first steam railway in England was around 1825 and that was probably just a few years before they were started in France.'

This observation did not seem to interest Monsieur Martin, who slightly raised his eyebrows and looked pained. I could have bitten off my tongue for starting the interview off on the wrong foot by bringing attention to any technical advance of

78

the British over the French, even though the event in question happened over 150 years ago.

'Well,' continued my visitor, 'with the advent of the railways it was considered wise to form a railway police.'

'Like in England,' I replied. 'Britain has railway policemen too.'

Monsieur Martin chose to ignore this comment and continued his discourse by saying that it was realised by the powers that were at that time that railways were facilitating communication and that the railway police could carry out other functions as well as policing the railway system.

'Such as?' I queried.

'Such as being aware of what was happening within the country: being aware of political or criminal activity.'

'Is there much difference?' I quipped, my Liverpool humour getting the better of me.

Monsieur Martin did not smile.

I began to understand that les Renseignements Généraux were in fact a sort of internal spy network attempting to keep relevant government services aware of any movement that could be considered subversive, or for that matter against the interest of whatever political party was in power at any particular time. Not nice, I thought. However, not wanting to appear difficult to Monsieur Martin, I turned the conversation to the subject of Paris. Knowing that one of the best ways to a Frenchman's heart is to emphasise the wonders of that city, I extolled its beauty.

'There is no doubt,' I said. 'Paris is certainly one of the most beautiful cities in the world, if not the most beautiful.'

Monsieur Martin smiled and I felt he was warming to me at last. Then I overdid it.

'In fact,' I said, 'it is so beautiful that it really belongs to the world. You French have an enormous responsibility in safe-guarding the beauty of such a city. It's a great pity that you have allowed fast food outlets to open on what is certainly the most beautiful avenue in the world. I refer, of course, to the Champs Elysées.'

Monsieur Martin hardened immediately and became very professional.

'What's the matter?' he demanded. 'Are you opposed to fast food outlets?'

'Good heavens no,' I hastened to reply. 'I just don't think that the Champs Elysées is really the best place for them. They don't give much added value to the beauty of the place.'

I felt I was screwing up my relationship with Monsieur Martin and I could tell that he was beginning to believe that he was dealing with some sort of Anglo-Saxon subversive pinko probably involved in all sorts of terrorist plots to blow up McDonald's, to mention just one. He ended our interview by suggesting that his service could be useful to me as a factory manager and that I could be useful to him.

'How's that?' I asked.

'Well, if you have any people problems or troublemakers, we could discuss them.'

'I'll certainly think about that,' I said. 'However, I think I can handle all the problems I have at the moment, although God knows there are a lot of them.'

On that note we shook hands again and Monsieur Martin left me. When he was gone, I sat and wondered on this French phenomenon of informing on one's neighbour. It had to be a result of an ingrained insecurity. Once again I felt sure that the Frenchman thought that by ingratiating himself with whatever authority was currently in power he was protecting his family and himself from future hassle and trouble. Whatever the reason, I was still British enough to view all forms of informing as distasteful.

6

STILL MAKING POP

During the time I spent managing the bottling factory I came both to like and respect the French worker. Despite the fact that French history is a long chain of disasters which were usually provoked by the contempt and betrayal demonstrated to the population by the ruling classes, the French worker is still, amazingly, prepared to have confidence in his manager. At least so it appeared to me, but perhaps the fact that I was not French gave me more credibility than I deserved. The French worker, I found, reacts positively to a challenge and is ready to believe the promises made to him by his boss. The inherently suspicious attitude that the French demonstrated in most of their relationships did not seem to apply to the same degree in the work context and, providing the promises I made were honoured – and they could be small promises – then the workers in the factory were prepared to go to great lengths to achieve the objectives that they were set. An approachable and stable management structure apparently gave the reassurance, both for the present and the future, that the French seem to need so much. The key word is 'approachable' because being able to speak freely to the factory manager was obviously a new experience for the workforce in general. Previously they had been subjugated to a formal French management which placed a virtually insurmountable barrier between the worker and the *cadre*. Once, when talking to a factory engineer on ways of improving a particular job on the bottling line, I advised him first to talk to the operator who was performing the task. The engineer looked at me in amazement before telling me that as he was a qualified engineer he certainly understood the task better than the person who was performing it.

Despite working for over 20 years in France, I have never really understood the title *'cadre'*. It carries with it numerous fringe benefits, pension rights etc. and normally is only applied to a manager who has a diploma or some higher-education qualification. However, with typical French inconsistency, there are both managers and qualified personnel who are not *cadres* and there are *cadres* who are not managers. It is a concept foreign to the British and acts in fact as a class barrier that has the negative effect of making it virtually impossible for any worker to be promoted above a certain level. Consequently, in French industry as in French politics there are very few leaders who have dirtied their hands in the rough and tumble of working life. The wide gap in culture between those who govern and those who are governed is perhaps one of the biggest obstacles that France will have to overcome if it is ever to become politically stable or to maintain its place in today's competitive industrial world.

In the factory the greatest difficulty lay in convincing the middle management of *cadres* to accept the idea of worker participation in team working, when the whole concept of a team is completely contrary to French culture. Given a problem to solve, the French manager usually expects to be left alone to solve it. He will not seek advice from anyone else, believing that if he cannot solve the problem himself this somehow reflects negatively upon his intelligence. Neither will he easily accept a deadline, considering that the solving of a problem will take whatever time is necessary and this cannot be identified before the problem is solved. This approach is diametrically opposite to that of an Anglo-Saxon manager, who when given a problem will first ask by when it has to be solved and then enumerate the assistance he needs to complete the task in the allotted time, automatically creating a team.

When through argument and coercion the middle management did agree to try and work to a new, for them, concept and within a new structure, productivity, which in the past had been an unknown word in the factory, began to improve. There was an air of confidence growing within the workforce, although it was evident that the shop stewards did not know how to react to the new culture. It was rewarding working in close relationship with the French shopfloor personnel, the dose of Latin temperament in their characters made it possible to appeal to their hearts as well as their brains and I was convinced that the factory could be turned into a highly succesful operation. However, I suspected that should I fail to deliver on my promises, then this same workforce would very quickly erect a guillotine in the factory yard. The French tend to be erratic and although capable of high achievements they are light on tenacity and can quickly become dispirited and discontented if their hopes are disappointed. Happily at that moment the expanding soft drink market, combined with the French willingness to work hard, was bringing in excellent results.

A potential pitfall to good relations in France lies in the custom of shaking people's hands each day at the first contact with them. During the early hours of each shift I made a habit of touring the factory, having a word or two with each operator and shaking their hand. The problem lay in the fact that most of the shopfloor workers, and there were roughly 100 of them at any one time, didn't stay in the same place but moved around the factory floor and it was difficult for me to remember with whom I had shaken hands and with whom I hadn't. This was a situation fraught with the risk of a social gaffe, because forgetting to shake someone's hand left them with the impression that you were deliberately ignoring them and they felt hurt, suspecting that they were out of favour. On the contrary, shaking a person's hand twice offended because the individual would reply, 'We have already shaken hands, don't you remember me?' In these cases my apologies, combined with my explanation that the English only shake hands at weddings and funerals, was usually accepted with good grace. Falling back on my Englishness often helped in similar difficult situations because the French seemed ready to accept that being English excused the most bizarre behaviour.

Felipe, of course, would not admit to my face that I was having any measure of success. 'I have sat in on some of your works meetings,' he told me. 'The only reason that you have not had a strike is because the shop steward doesn't understand a word of what you are saying. You speak to them in your indescribably bad French and the shop steward pretends to be intelligent enough to understand you: so he nods his head in agreement without having the faintest clue as to what the hell you are talking about.' Such a comment was about par for Felipe, who never praised anyone to their face but who would show his appreciation in other ways, such as in a salary increase, which was one of the things I liked about him.

'O speak to reassure me'
John Ernest Bode: 'O Jesus I have promised', hymn, 1869

Above all, the Frenchman seeks reassurance. Tell a Frenchman that his country is wonderful, that Paris is the most beautiful city in the world, that French cusine is fabulous and that you find him intelligent, and he is already prepared to hold you in high regard. Here he differs considerably from the British. Tell a Briton that his country is in a terrible state and rapidly going to the dogs and he will probably agree with you. However, the probable reason why the Briton and particularly the Englishman feels at liberty to decry his country is that he is so firmly convinced that England and all things English are second to none that he does not require any assurance from anyone to confirm his opinion. While in terms of enriching his culture it might be unfortunate that the Englishman holds this point of view, it does give him a terrible strength. I remember that during the war years a certain William Joyce, better known as 'Lord Haw-Haw', broadcast each evening from Hamburg. This was an English language propaganda programme aimed at destroying the morale of the British. So far as my family were concerned, and it was surely true for most if not all of Britain, it was second only to Tommy Handley's *ITMA* in entertainment value. As a propagandist Mr Joyce was wasting his time, but he could probably have made a fortune as a radio comedian. There was no way my father would miss his programme. At the appointed hour the radio would be turned on and he would listen attentively, chuckling to himself at what he considered to be the absurdities of 'Lord Haw-Haw'. Unlike the French, the British have no need for reassurance in the destiny of their country and there was absolutely no reason why Authority should have even tried to jam the broadcast. Poor William Joyce was hanged as a traitor at the end of the war, a sentence which many in Britain felt was unfair considering the amusement he had provided.

In the working environment the French need for reassurance is also evident. A person's job title is virtually of equal importance to them as their salary. Technical and administrative staff are happiest in their own individual office, the Frenchman above all is an individualist and as such does not take easily either to team working or to open-plan offices. Once in his own office, the Frenchman will keep the door closed, and should there be an interior window he will, given the chance, immediately cover it with a technical drawing or a number of notices or anything else that comes readily to hand to screen him from external view. Finally, cocooned in his own closed office and with an impressive job title, he feels reassured that he is an indispensable part of the organisation.

'None will sweat but for promotion'
William Shakespeare: *As You Like It*

In 1983 Felipe became General Manager of the French company and I replaced him as Technical Director. This promotion gave me exposure to a completely different aspect of French working life. Firstly my new position was located in the head office in central Paris and secondly I now also took responsibility for the company's other factory, which was in a small village close to Marseilles.

It was my first close contact with the people of the south of France. Unlike their Parisian colleagues, the workers in the southern factory were not associated to any trade union. The workforce consisted mainly of three distinctive cultural groups. There were the local indigenous French, steeped in the agricultural culture of the Midi, and there were also many *pieds noirs*; these were the ex-colonials who had been born in North Africa and had returned to France, often penniless, following the independence of the French territories. Lastly, there was a high proportion of immigrants from Italy and Spain. The combination of these three distinctive cultures made an amalgam difficult to manage. The *pieds noirs* in particular proved to be extremely individualistic, and if the concept of team working was difficult to realise in the Parisian factory, it was almost impossible in its southern counterpart. Jealous undercurrents ran through the organisation and internal politics were rife.

I cannot say that I really enjoyed working with this mixture of people from the south. I found many of them to be small-minded and, although polite and friendly to one's face, rather insincere. Neither did I care much for their climate; visits to the south during the summer months would make me feel thirsty for the trees. To see the grass burned by the sun and the parched soil made me long for the green pastures of the north. It was nevertheless an ideal climate for the sale of soft drinks.

However, being based in the head office in central Paris was a joy. It was located in the eighth arrondissement, an area with wide boulevards, busy restaurants and cafés, a park and impressive buildings. A stone's throw from the Champs Elysées, I became particularly attached to it.

One morning Michel, the head of the buying department, which in my new position was under my responsibility, put his head around my office door and asked me if I had any plans for lunch. When I replied that I was free he asked me if I would care to join him as he was having lunch with a rep from a potential supplier. 'It's a woman and quite an attractive one, and what's more she says she knows you,' he told me. Intrigued, I followed him to a nearby restaurant to find, sitting at the table waiting for us, Jocelyne.

Some ten years had passed since I had last seen her but she was still pretty in her maturity, with eyes still as green as I remembered them. I felt a resurgence of the feelings that I had once had for her and was glad of Michel's presence because it kept the conversation restricted to business, only allowing the occasional reference between Jocelyne and myself to our past friendship. Over lunch I did discover that she was now married, the mother of two little boys and living happily in a suburb to the west of Paris. It was a good lunch, offered by Jocelyne on behalf of her company, but I left the table feeling very much older.

Dreams of Retirement

I was approaching my fifty-sixth birthday and my eventual retirement was something I began to consider. Although I had travelled fairly extensively in France, it had mainly been between cities and I had not found the countryside in which I would like to retire. Suggestions to Annie that upon retirement we would go and live in England were not met with much enthusiasm. Nevertheless, I had an idea that we could buy a cottage somewhere in the Cotswolds, an area in which I had once lived and had since believed to be one of the most pleasant parts of England.

My memories of the Cotswolds dated from the late 1960s and subsequent visits there in the 1980s disappointed me. The English, as is their tendency, seemed to have turned the entire Cotswold area into a theme park. Gone were the small country villages of agricultural workers with their post offices and their cider-smelling pubs. In their place blossomed ye olde tea shoppes, antique shops and farms converted into holiday flatlets. The villages were spoiled through being immaculately manicured and the remaining country pubs had car parks full of BMWs and Porsches. We had the impression that we were visiting a corner of Disneyland and decided that it was not for us.

Annie and I spent many months discussing where we would

like to make our future home and during that time made
holiday visits to various parts of France. Annie wanted the
sun, but I was sure that after my working experiences I would
not be able to settle in the south of France. We looked at
Brittany, which I liked but Annie found too wet. We looked
at Alsace, which I also liked but Annie found too cold.
Eventually, after a holiday in the south-west of France, an
area which combines both sun and greenery, we agreed that it
was there that we would like to live. In a small village in the
Landes we purchased a large old house dating from 1790 and
badly in need of restoration. Our idea was to use it as a
holiday home until such time as I retired.

Robbery and Bureaucracy

Meanwhile the company continued its healthy expansion rate
and in 1987 Felipe was promoted to the position of the
company's European President. He was now responsible for
the company's business in most of Europe with the exception
of the UK, which for some reason seldom seems to be included
as part of Europe. Felipe was replaced in France by a new
General Manager, François, and it was during the time that I
worked for him that I was to be the principal player in a
drama that could not have illustrated more clearly the enormous cultural gap that lies between the French and the
English.

Along with François, the Personnel and Marketing Directors
and 80 salesmen, I was present at a three-day sales conference
which took place in London. These affairs tend to be noisy,
exhilarating and wild; over the convention period the sales
force gradually works itself up into a mild frenzy as it con-
vinces itself that it is the finest sales force that ever existed.
The emotion is carried over into the evenings and after the
second hectic night out in London the Marketing Director and
I decided that we would take the last night, which was a
Friday, more easily and return to the hotel before midnight.
We did this, but stayed at the hotel bar for some time and I

finally went up to my bedroom on the fifth floor in the early hours of Saturday morning. Tired and with a little too much alcohol in my system, I was quickly into bed and asleep, only to be awakened before dawn by a tremendous banging on the door. Staggering to the door and opening it, I was confronted by a policeman holding in his hand a rather dirty blue shirt.

'Is this your shirt, sir?' he enquired.

I gazed at him with incomprehension for a moment before telling him to 'sod off', adding that I was not in the mood to put up with a drunken salesman making a practical joke at this god-forsaken hour of the morning.

The policeman remained adamant and calmly repeated his question. I then perceived, hovering in the background, another personage dressed in the manner of a hotel manager. I examined the shirt more closely and finally agreed that it did indeed look like one of mine.

'Would you mind,' said the policeman, 'looking to see if anything else is missing from your room.'

I only wear a pyjama top in bed, and as well as thinking that I looked foolish standing there, I also became aware of a rather cold, unpleasant breeze circulating around my nether regions. I turned my head towards the interior of the room and saw that the window was wide open. Now alarmed but still half believing that I was the victim of a salesman's joke, I opened the wardrobe door, only to find it as bare as Mother Hubbard's cupboard. I had been visited by a cat burglar, and the only possession he or she had left me was the pyjama top I was wearing.

Things then happened very quickly. I immediately telephoned to Annie at home and asked her to put a stop on credit cards and chequebook. That settled, my friend and colleague the Personnel Director was able to lend me all the clothing necessary, but unfortunately he was much smaller than I in height and rather larger around the midriff. Still, at least I was dressed. The next problem to sort out was how I was going to return to France on that Saturday evening flight without a passport. I tried ringing the British Embassy but was informed that the passport office was closed on a Saturday and

89

that I would have to present myself on Monday morning. Every avenue I tried in London met me with the same response: 'Sorry we are closed, call back on Monday.'

It was François who had the answer: 'There is no point in trying to do anything in England on a Saturday,' he said. 'Ring the British Embassy in Paris.' I followed his advice and entered into a long struggle via Paris with various British organisations in London, including, I suspect, MI5. I told countless lies in giving the reasons why it was imperative that I returned to France that day. I described the fragile state of my heart, which, I claimed, needed constant treatment in France and eventually I managed to equip myself with an official-looking paper requesting that French Immigration allow me to enter France even though I was without a passport. My question to the British Immigration officer at Heathrow as to the value of the document for getting me into France was met with: 'I don't know if it will get you into France, but it will get you out of England.'

'Thanks,' I replied.

François, the Personnel Director, and I took our scheduled flight from Heathrow to Charles De Gaulle, and once there debated on the question of how to handle the French Immigration Police. We aimed for a young, friendly-looking officer at the passport barrier and decided that François would pass first and that I would follow him, while the Personnel Manager would bring up the rear. François approached the barrier and presented his passport for inspection in the usual manner. I followed immediately behind him

'Passport,' demanded the officer, without much of a look in my direction. I handed him the paper which the UK immigration services had kindly provided for me. The French official glanced at it and then he looked at me. Doing a double take, he examined me more closely. The trouser legs of my suit came to somewhere around mid-calf, the jacket hung loosely across my midriff, while its sleeves ended nearer to my elbows than to my wrists. The officer raised his eyebrows and handed me back my paper. 'Passport,' he demanded again.

I had decided that the best thing I could do was to keep my

mouth closed and say nothing. I again gave the paper to the officer. 'Passport,' he demanded for the third time. I again motioned to the paper. The officer then turned to an older and probably senior colleague and showed him the paper. This gentleman threw one glance at the paper and another glance at the length of my trouser legs and said, '*C'est un Anglais, laisse passer.*' I hurried past the barrier into the anonymity of the arrival hall as quickly as possible, but the immigration officer must have had second thoughts because he arrested the Personnel Director who had been hard on my heels.

The story has a sequel. The following morning was a Sunday and Annie and I went to the local gendarmerie to declare the theft of my driving licence and resident's permit. The young gendarme loaded his typewriter with a blank form and then began all the inevitable questions concerning the marital state of my long-deceased grandmother, God rest her soul. All was proceding normally if somewhat slowly until he asked me where my papers had been stolen. When I replied London, the gendarme immediately stopped his one-finger typing exercise.

'I can't help you,' he said.

'Why not?' I asked.

'Because as your papers were stolen in a foreign country, you must make your declaration there,' he said.

'I already did,' I replied, and then added, 'Look, I know what is going to happen. I'm going to have to get a copy of the declaration that I made to the London police and then I'm going to have to have it translated into French and the whole thing is going to take months and months. I need a duplicate driving licence quickly. Please advise me what is the best thing for me to do. I do love living in France but please help me to avoid all the bureacracy that is about to be unleashed on my head.'

'Right,' said the gendarme. 'You did not have your papers stolen, you lost them and you don't know where.'

This was '*Système D*' at its best. 'Indeed,' I said. 'Absolutely correct and thank you very much.'

With that, the gendarme threaded another form into his

typewriter, completed his paperwork and within three weeks I had had my duplicate driving licence and resident's permit. Life is not complicated in France, once you know the rules.

Spanish Interlude – 1

In 1987 the company was investing very heavily in the States and had decided that as the Americans were the undisputed kings of soft drinks, they would place the overall Continental European business under their sphere of influence. Felipe, meanwhile, had in some way convinced the Americans that Barcelona was the centre of Europe and as a result obtained their agreement that it was a logical place to situate the main European headquarters. Following his move to Barcelona, Felipe offered me the post of Technical Vice President Europe, which I accepted with pleasure, and leaving the responsibility of renovating our future retirement home in Annie's capable hands I relocated to Barcelona.

The American management proved difficult. I believe that American businessmen responsible for overseas operations fall into two main categories. There are those who have long experience in working internationally and generally make excellent managers and there are the homespun Americans who have had no previous experience of working internationally and seem to see no cultural difference between Paris, Texas and Paris, France. Unfortunately in our case we mainly inherited the latter and only one or two of the former. Eventually one came to accept the telephone calls at all hours, the time differential between the two continents being ignored or forgotten, and the questions of whether or not Brussels and Marseilles were in the same country. These were only minor irritations. The most irritating aspect of the homespun American was his unshakeable conviction that whatever sold succesfully in the States would also suceed anywhere else. Consequently it was difficult, for instance, to convince them that a raspberry-flavoured, over-sweet ginger drink would almost certainly not meet the French or Spanish expectations for a soft drink, despite the fact that it was going 'gangbusters' in downtown New York. The Americans would continue in their convictions, and although it is true to say that they have been remarkably successful in exporting their non-culture across a wide spectrum of activities to most parts of the world without firing a single shot in anger, rasperry-flavoured ginger ale is still a non-runner in France.

Established in Barcelona, or as the Americans said, with their ability to crucify the English language and communicate with as few words as possible, 'officing' out of Barcelona on a cross-frontier basis with most of the western Europe countries, I began to see the French through the eyes of the Germans and the Spanish. They, along with the English and the Belgians, all seemed to find the French a difficult people to deal with, and to me this attitude seemed to be in contradiction to their holiday habits. Many English, Germans and Belgians apparently love to visit France – it is one of their most popular foreign destinations for holidays and thousands of them buy houses in the Dordogne and Normandy. Yet many of them will say that although France is a beautiful country they do not appreciate the French people. I find this a strange comment. Why, one might ask, do they love France? If it is for the climate, then both Italy and Spain have a better one and they are both cheaper places either to live or to holiday. If it is for the coastline or countryside, then Italy also has a beautiful countryside and beaches, while Spain has magnificent beaches. So what is the great attraction of France? It is probable that the Anglo-Saxon is attracted to the French way of life and it seems incongruous to say that one loves a certain way of life but dislikes the people that created it.

While it may be true that the French are complicated both in their thinking and in their actions, I did not find adapting to life in France any more difficult than adapting to Spain during the time I lived and worked there. Neither did I experience any great difficulty in working with the French, once I had begun to understand their culture and gain their confidence. To the contrary, in the main I found the French workers to be enthusiastic and willing to make extraordinary efforts to

93

succeed in their objectives. They do not suffer from the rigid discipline that constipates the Germans, neither do they have the insularity of the Spanish, who often readily agree with a proposition while their main concern is that you will kindly go away as quickly as possible and leave them alone.

It was 1988, and a large part of the industrial world was anxiously preparing for the magic date of 1991 when the European frontiers were scheduled to disappear. Various consultants were making small fortunes advising industry on the steps that they needed to take to ensure that their business would survive and be successful in the new Europe. Our American management were convinced that this wonder-working date would see the foundation of the United States of Europe and suggested that we build a factory midway between France and Spain to supply both countries with soft drinks. The fact that such a location would be in the centre of the Pyrenees did not totally exclude it from their consideration. In the event, the date came and went without a bang or a whimper so far as we were concerned, which meant that either we were well prepared for it or the consultants had been deluding us with a paper tiger.

Barcelona was throbbing with preparations for the Olympics, but by 1989 I suspected that the Americans were beginning to question whether or not Barcelona was really the potential business capital of Europe. Such thoughts did not worry me too much. My retirement was rapidly approaching and I was finishing my career on a high note.

7

SPANISH INTERLUDE

I enjoyed my years in Barcelona, where the lifestyle suited me even more than in France. I had a large apartment within a ten-minute walk of our new offices and would start each day with a light breakfast of toast and a fresh orange juice before walking briskly along the wide pavements to the office. The warmth of the morning sun, the clear blue sky and the sight of the attractive Spanish girls hurrying to work gave me a feeling of well-being and a readiness to face whatever the day had in store. Once inside the office, however, the atmosphere was somewhat different. In furnishing the place, Felipe had given free reign to an interior office designer who I often thought must have been taking opium. All the furniture was black, the walls were grey and the soft furnishings deep blue. Colour psychology denotes black as negative, grey as an indeterminate colour with homosexual connotations, while blue is considered depressive. Is it any wonder, I would reflect at those times when business life was difficult and frustrating, that I sit here like a right wanker, unable to make a positive decision and feeling depressed? I never shared these thoughts with Felipe, who was exceedingly proud of the layout of his new office block.

The truth was that it was difficult to manage at a distance, and despite Felipe's insistence that Barcelona was the centre of European activity – a belief which, by the way, I only ever heard shared by his fellow Catalans – I was a long way from the European production units. My role as a European Vice President was to try and coordinate these far-flung units into an effective European operation, and as they were mainly located in Paris, Hamburg and Madrid a great deal of travelling was involved.

After spending my first week in my new job wondering how, sitting in an office in Barcelona with my mind in neutral, I could possibly become an effective European manager, I arrived at what I thought could be a viable solution. I allocated the study of different aspects of production, such as quality, productivity and logistics, to multinational teams with each team under the leadership of a different country. These study teams were to recommend changes to improve existing working practices in their disciplines, which, if agreed by the relevant general manager of the country concerned, would be implemented by these same teams. This idea, simple though it was, seemed to please everybody and as a consequence, given that it had the support of the general managers, it began to work and give some positive results. The idea was also instrumental in breaking through national insularity and provided me with a cross-frontier base upon which I could start to build a European framework. I had hit upon a 'win–win idea', everybody was happy, each country was contributing and each country was in turn benefiting. I had one of those rare moments in life of feeling pleased with myself when some months later the European Marketing Vice President, whose office was adjacent to mine, introduced the same idea in marketing.

Outside the working environment it was the night life that attracted me most to Barcelona. Leaving the office late in the evening, I would stop for a beer at a local bodega and then busy myself around the apartment until nine or ten at night. At this hour Barcelona became alive. The streets started to become crowded and the restaurants opened their doors. Eating out before ten at night was considered early and the restaurants only began to fill around midnight. Barcelona would stay noisy and active well into the early hours of the morning, the pavement cafés and bars crowded. It was a mystery to me how the Spaniard's constitution could cope with such early morning revelry and still permit him to be at work not much later on the same morning. The health fanatics of the north would prophesy an early death for all of them.

I enjoyed Spanish food, and still do. It does not have the sophistication of French cuisine – the Spanish are light on sauces – but the quality of the produce used is superb. Even in Madrid, which is about as far from the sea that one can get in Spain, the fish dishes taste as if the fish have just swum into the kitchen, while the seafood everywhere is superb. How the Spanish manage to serve huge quantities of sea-fresh fish and seafood over 200 miles inland is a logistical enigma that I have never been able to fathom, but they do.

The Spanish experience was a satisfactory finish to my career, or at least I expected it to be so, having agreed with Felipe that I would take early retirement at the end of 1989. My replacement had been identified, and in the September of that year began arranging the relocation of his family and himself to Barcelona. I was looking forward to being reunited with Annie and starting a new life in the French countryside. The renovation of our house in Duhort-Bachen was nearing completion and Annie was in the process of achieving a remarkable transformation, installing modern appliances where needed but retaining and even accentuating the charm of the original building. However, as the poet said, 'The best laid schemes o' mice an' men gang aft a-gley' and all that. Events within the French company were to change my plans.

Back to Paris

Towards the end of the summer of 1989 I was due to attend a management meeting in Hamburg, and once Marisa, my charming and efficient Andalusian secretary, had furnished me with all the necessary travel tickets and hotel reservation, I left the office for Barcelona airport. There being no direct flight from Barcelona to Hamburg, I had to change planes at Paris, Charles De Gaulle. Arriving there and faced with an hour or so of kicking my heels while waiting for the Lufthansa connecting flight to Hamburg, I wandered over to the nearest bar for a little light refreshment and walked into François, the General Manager of the French company. We were both scheduled to be at the Hamburg meeting and were both booked on the same flight out of Charles De Gaulle. I liked François and had worked for him before my promotion to Barcelona. He had been instrumental in getting me back into France after the trauma of my London robbery, and the memory of this painful episode always gave him a laugh. He had even turned it into one of his favourite after-dinner stories. I was always pleased to see François and we had a drink together before making our way to the departure lounge to join the flight.

Upon boarding the plane I was faced with one of those embarrassing moments which unfortunately we are all bound to experience from time to time in our lives. Marisa, always conscious of her self-imposed duty to consider my status, had, despite my protestations about needless expense, booked me into first class while François, always conscious of the need to economise, had booked business class. Consequently, whereas I was ushered into one of Luthansa's deep leather armchairs, François was perched behind the curtain a few rows behind me. Fortunately the flight was far from full, and as there was a vacant perch next to François, I forsook my armchair and moved to sit beside him, feeling embarrassed at the apparent extravagance of European head office personnel in contrast to the cost-saving attitude of those at the sharp end of the business. The matter could have ended there, but I had forgotten German discipline. There followed fairly heated words between the steward and myself. He insisted that as I had a first-class ticket I must sit in the first-class compartment, while I tried to reason with him, explaining that I wished to discuss business matters with a colleague. Eventually the steward left us, but with his German sense of hierarchical order obviously affronted. Later, when a meal was served the steward plonked a glass of champagne and a dish of smoked salmon firmly down in front of me, with a look that said you are going to have that whether you like it or not; while a little later, and with a condescending air, François was handed a sausage and a couple of cold potatoes. I offered my champagne to François, who refused it, and as I felt guilty drinking it alone it remained in front of us, in silent accusation of head office expense, for the remainder of the flight.

The champagne incident apart, the flight was pleasant enough. During our conversation François explained that he had a staff problem because his Operations Director had left the company fairly suddenly and he now needed time to recruit another one. He asked me if I would be prepared to delay my retirement for a few months and return to France, taking on the position on a purely temporary basis. I was not wholly opposed to the idea and we agreed to discuss the matter further in Paris the following week.

The discussions we held in Paris resulted in my return to the French company under favourable conditions. I negotiated that I would stay in a hotel within walking distance of the French offices from Monday to Friday and return home by air to the south-west of France each weekend. My hotel was in the rue de Rocher in the *huitième Arrondissement*, a district which still remains unspoiled by development. The area around the hotel contains two theatres and the almost adjacent Parc Monceau offers the opportunity either for a stroll among the greenery or for any other exercise that one might feel inclined to take. The nearby rue de Lévis holds a daily busy street market and the wide boulevard des Batignolles, lined with numerous restaurants to suit all pockets, points arrow straight to the Place de Clichy and reveals the white dome of Sacré Coeur on the skyline. The whole area has remained in a time warp and is little changed from the Paris I knew in my student days. It was and still is the Paris of a bygone time. The hotel is itself of very recent construction, although as the original façade had been left in place and the hotel constructed behind it the harmony with the other buildings had not been destroyed. This hotel was to be my Parisian home and I soon became friendly with Allan, one of the receptionists.

There was no doubt as to Allan's origin. He is the only person that I have ever met who speaks near-perfect French with a strong Liverpool accent. He had arrived in Paris some

99

years previously as a member of what must have been a rather unsuccessful pop group. Awaking one morning in the small hotel where they were staying, he discovered that overnight the group had become a solo act and that he was left to pay the bill. After living rough in Paris for a few weeks, he had found work in the hotel business, where his English, despite an accent you could cut with a knife, was an asset. Meeting with a fellow Liverpudlian gave me a partner with whom I could share the special humour of that city which I had left some 40 years previously. Allan and I would laugh together over jokes incomprehensible to the other receptionists, Marie and Pierre, despite their excellent command of the English language. Nevertheless, they would listen to us and smile politely whenever we tried to explain a Liverpool joke to them.

The hospitality shown to me by the staff and the cleanliness of the hotel itself made my stay there very pleasant, which was just as well because the few months that François had allowed himself to find my replacement proved to be a delusion. His recruitment plans had been complicated by the fact that at that time the company had begun negotiations for the purchase of another large French soft drinks business which was to be integrated into the existing French operation. The associated long-term investment and human complications decided François to maintain as much stability as possible within his own management team, so any changes that he could avoid were out of the question. My planned few months' stay was to develop into two years.

Working with François was both rewarding and interesting. He was a generous boss and, unlike many of the French managers that I had encountered, he was approachable and a great believer in delegation. The potential purchase was to more than double his number of factories and to greatly increase the French production capability, while for me the challenge of incorporating such a large addition of personnel into the company was as exciting as the large amount of engineering that needed to be undertaken.

It was towards the end of 1991 when François and I agreed

that it was the right time for me to finally retire. Fond farewells, with all the usual trimmings, were made and for the last time I braved the frenetic Friday Parisian traffic to make my way to Orly airport and catch the late evening flight to Pau. Annie met me at the airport, as she had done every Friday night for the past two years. We drove into Pau and dined at our favourite fish restaurant, finishing the evening by sharing a celebratory bottle of champagne with our Egyptian friend Yhab, the proprietor of the restaurant. Later that night Annie drove the 55 kilometres back to our newly restored house in Duhort-Bachen, the small Landaise village which was our home. I was finally retired and, full of anticipation for a new life in the beautiful countryside of deepest France, I went to bed and slept well.

8

DUHORT – 1

Duhort-Bachen, or more simply just Duhort, as it is locally known, is a tiny village in south-west France on the borders of the *départements* of Landes and Gers. It is situated halfway between the small, pretty town of Airè-sur-l'Adour and the spa village of Eugénie les Bains. It is here at Eugénie that one of the most celebrated French chefs specialises in serving exquisite low-calorie dishes to the discerning visitor in search of health. Here magic spells are woven daily as loss of weight becomes possible with gourmet food and without the misery of an insipid diet.

Duhort itself is little more than a square bounded by trees and to arrive there is to be already at its centre. The principal buildings consist of a church, a school, the *mairie*, a water-mill and, of course, a restaurant. In fact all that is needed for a happy and contented life. Our house fronted directly on to the narrow pavement and looked through the trees and across the grass of the square to the restaurant half hidden beneath its arcades. The back of the house gave on to a half-acre of mature garden, which in turn led on to a field and then forest.

The Landes forms part of Aquitaine, and with over 9,000 square kilometres is the second largest *département* of France. Up to the nineteenth century this vast expanse remained mainly marshland, and although Napoleon Bonaparte had intentions to develop the area his unfortunate experience at Waterloo put paid to any plans he might have had in that direction. It was not until the mid-nineteenth century, and with the support of his nephew, that well-meaning but ineffectual emperor Louis Napoleon, that the area was reclaimed. Canals were dug and one of the largest forests in Europe planted. The flat land was drained, and these days tourists who take pleasure in the 100 kilometres of clean sandy coast and its surfable Atlantic breakers may well find the endless straight roads that cut through the pine forests a monotonous drive. Duhort, however, far inland and bordering between the Landes and the green undulating countryside of the Gers, nestles snugly in a valley.

Although internally the house had been completely restored, some work was still required to the exterior – and that was to be our next and final project. Locally there were excellent and obliging craftsmen and we were very pleased with the quality of the work they had done for us, so as soon as we felt financially able and ready to start work on the outside of the house we contacted our builder friend, Philippe.

It was late in the afternoon of a sunny midsummer Friday that Philippe, after a polite knock on the open front door, strolled into the house and at our invitation settled himself down in the lounge to enjoy a little aperitif while we outlined, rather vaguely, our thoughts for restoring the front of the house. We knew from experience that he would be able to develop our rough ideas into a number of realisable alternatives and give us quick but fairly reliable cost estimates for each of them to help us make a decision. After the usual exchange of family news and of events in and around the village, we finished our aperitifs and then Philippe and I wandered out on to the pavement to study in more detail the old but rather dilapidated front of the house.

We were busily engaged in conversation when the students arrived. Their minibus, announcing in large letters on its side that it belonged to a learning facility in Grimsby, hesitatingly navigated a first circuit of the village square. On its second circuit it stopped in front of Philippe and myself just as we were discussing the merits of different treatments to enhance the stone façade of the house. A head extended from the vehicle and requested, in broken French and a broad Lincoln-shire accent, directions to the local *gîte*. My reply in English caused a laugh among the students crammed into the trans-port, to the apparent discomfort of the said head, which later

103

proved to belong to the 'Prof'. Directions being given, the minibus departed to the other side of the square, with Philippe only remarking to me '*Ils sont les Anglais*',' before the village returned to its normal somnolent state.

Normality reigned until early Sunday afternoon. I was surveying the garden weeds proliferating in the sun when my wife, disturbing me with her charming if very occasionally defective English, informed me that *Monsieur le forgeron*, the village blacksmith, better known in the village as 'Bikini', was at the door in a highly excited state and needed my immediate assistance. I have to admit that I had great difficulty with Bikini's accent, which is deep south-west France, and it was even almost unintelligible to Annie, who after all is French, albeit Parisian. Listening with great concentration to Bikini's rapid-fire speech, I began to understand that the problem, whatever it was, seemed to be centred at Les Arcades, the local *auberge*, and it apparently concerned 'les Anglais'. Fearing the worst and with a quick 'I'll be back in a minute' to Annie, I accompanied Bikini across the square to the bar in question.

The first problem was easy to resolve. The Prof having left for Bordeaux airport to collect a further batch of students, those remaining had settled themselves happily in the bar and thought it would be a good idea if they were to collect their cassette player from the *gîte* and enliven the bar with some music. They only wanted to know if *le patron* would be in agreement with such a move. Unfortunately he was not, and I duly informed the students of his decision. If the students accepted *le patron*'s refusal, Bikini didn't. Once he had understood the request and its refusal, he decided to take the matter into his own hands and organise the afternoon's entertainment for the students. It was really from this point that the whole thing went out of control.

'*Tous le monde chez moi*,' he exclaimed. '*Au forge!*'

It is necessary at this stage to explain that Bikini's forge is more a centre of social activity than a forge, and that while he does not involve himself with too much smithy work these days, he has installed his wine barrels there, each barrel filled

104

with his own home-produced wine and each having one or two glasses, probably last washed during the reign of Louis Napoleon and deeply encrusted with wine deposit, balanced on top of them. The students, amongst whom there were some pretty girls, were delighted with this development, as were one or two of the local youths who had happened to join us in our short walk across the square to the forge. Plastic goblets appeared to join Bikini's glasses and everyone drank everyone else's health. One of the students then mentioned to me that they intended to prepare an evening meal for the returning Prof and the newly arriving students. Potatoes and onions were needed for the recipe, so did I know where such items could be procured locally on a Sunday afternoon? By this time I had become unofficial interpreter for the group and I made known the enquiry.

'*Mais oui, bien sûr,*' volunteered one of the locals. '*Venez avec moi.*'

Knowing France well enough to suspect the probable outcome of such an excursion, I dragged one of the students with me. He was hopefully to be my future excuse for an early return and the three of us piled into the local's 2 CV, a vehicle of uncertain age. Off we drove into deepest France. Our driver, who introduced himself as Henri, informed us that we were going to call at his aunt's smallholding and that she was certain to have a plentiful supply of potatoes and onions as well as the odd chicken or two if needed. We arrived there towards the end of the family's Sunday lunch and just in time to join them *au table* for a little armagnac. Beneath the hams strung along the overhead beams we drank to everyone's health and then to the village of Duhort and then to *les Anglais*, then to France and then to anyone else who came to mind. We finally left in the 2 CV with a plentiful supply of potatoes freely given in the interest of *l'entente cordiale*, but unfortunately without the onions as auntie did not have a sufficient quantity.

'*Ce n'est pas grave,*' said Henri, with whom we had by now pledged eternal friendship. 'I have a cousin, we will go to see him.'

I had been afraid of this sort of development but also knew that there was nothing I could politely do to change the course of events. Henri was obviously enjoying himself and the student would have tales to tell about life in the French countryside when he returned to Grimsby. I sat back and relaxed – with just a little concern about Annie, who would be wondering what had happened to me – and decided to let the events unfold. They were going to anyway.

We arrived at the cousin's farm late in the afternoon, to be met with the usual handshakes and a general bustle as space was cleared around the table.

'*Ils sont les Anglais*,' announced Henri, 'and they need some onions.'

'*Mais oui, mais oui, pas de problème, bien* sûr,' replied the cousin, and onions were swiftly forthcoming – as were glasses and pastis and the local aperitif, *floc*.

'*Préférez-vous le whisky*?' asked the cousin, and a bottle of Johnny Walker appeared.

When eventually we headed back towards the forge, the car was filled with sufficient potatoes and onions to feed the entire village and the student was in a deep sleep on the back seat.

Meanwhile, back in the forge, the party had grown to alarming proportions and we were obliged to join in a rugby scrum around the door in order to push our way into the interior, where I could see Bikini wreathed in smiles, leaning against one of the barrels and surrounded by students all drinking and acclaiming his wine and life in south-west France in general. Amongst the crowd were a number of gaily dressed youths in costumes akin to that of matadors. These were locals recently returned from the arena, where they had been actively participating in a *course landaise*, a hair-raising sport which mainly consists of jumping over a charging young cow. These village lads had of course collared the girls.

'*Eh! Monsieur, monsieur*, tell her I am a bullfighter,' one called to me. He was in deep conversation with a non-French-speaking Grimsby beauty who, judging by her reply, obviously didn't believe a word of my translation. The fact that none of the French understood English and none of the English under-

106

stood French did not seem in any way to detract from the earnestness of the conversations, and given that everyone was talking at the same time, any language difference seemed insignificant. One of the students had evidently returned to the *gîte* to collect the cassette player, which was adding rock music to the general noise. Bikini was filling plastic cups as fast as they were emptied and demanding that someone take photographs. It was now late in the evening and I thought that the best thing that I could do was to quietly disappear and return home. Unobtrusively, I left the forge reverberating to the sound of music and returned home to face the second problem that had now arisen that Sunday, explaining my five-hour absence to Annie.

Following this episode I became very friendly with Bikini, whose real name is Robert. Apparently he had earned his nickname because as a young man his favourite dance was named 'Le Bikini'. Robert is a bachelor who was nearing retirement at that time and living with his brother Pierre in a house they had inherited from their parents. By political persuasion Robert is a communist and we were to spend many hours sitting in the midst of his wine barrels discussing politics and history, once I had acclimatised to his accent, while lubricating our conversations with their contents. He is also an ecologist, using nothing but natural manure to fertilise the vines from which he makes his very drinkable local wine. To say that he keeps hens would be misleading, as they have the free range of the entire village and feed upon corn and whatever else they can scratch out of the ground. Needless to say, these hens produce eggs of a quality which I had forgotten existed, and although they are intended for his own consumption he would usually find me a few if I asked him. We would search together among the many nests that the hens had made around the forge until he found half a dozen still warm eggs for me. They were superb, with deep orange yolks and a taste that I vaguely remembered from my childhood years in the 1930s. They made many an excellent breakfast for Annie and me.

Robert is not a very active man and rarely leaves the village, except to tend his vines or once a month drive into the town of Airè sur l'Adour and visit the market or perhaps have a hair-cut. On these days he wears his suit and scrubs his face until it is shining, then with his beret set firmly on his head he climbs into his ancient Ami 6 Citroën and leaves the village. Apart from these excursions, he can be found most mornings engaged in some minor smithy work. In the afternoon, after having eaten his midday soup, always prepared and served by his brother Pierre, he usually sits in the sun and is always ready for a little conversation. On a Sunday afternoon he sometimes joins in with other villagers for a game of *pétanque*, which, apart from cultivating his vines, constitutes his only exercise.

One day, exploring the various sheds and barns littered around the forge, I noticed that he had two cars, both of the same 20-or-more-year-old model Ami 6, and both of a colour that had once been white.

'You evidently like white Citroëns,' I remarked, mainly just to start the conversation. 'Both your cars look the same.'

'It's not only the colour that's the same,' replied Robert. 'Have a look at the number plates.'

A glance at the number plates showed me that both cars had identical registration numbers. I looked at Robert who grinned at me and then I understood that even here in deepest France the same *Système D* was operating. Robert had the benefit of two cars for the cost of one insurance.

Robert's brother Pierre is an entirely different character and the only similarity they share is that they are both bachelors. Pierre earns his livelihood cultivating corn as well as keeping half a dozen cows, a couple of which Robert had trained to pull a plough across the fields before the corn-sowing seasons. Pierre's interest in the cows lies mainly in rearing their calves for veal. He is a typical hard-working *paysan*, his only relaxation being his passion for the local hunt.

In this region of the south-west hunting is mainly for wood pigeon and deer, with the occasional wild boar. The hunting of the wood pigeon in particular is clothed in custom and tradition. The hunters first construct a two-storey shelter in the forest, well camouflaged with branches and leaves, and then equip it with a table and chairs as well as, most importantly, a few bottles of armagnac. The final preparation is to attach a tame pigeon to the branch of a nearby tree by an ingenious system of string and wire, with one of the wires descending into the shelter. A slight pull on this wire gives the decoy pigeon the equivalent of a gentle kick in its posterior, causing it to flutter its wings. During this time the hopeful hunters are located on the top floor of the shelter with their guns pointing skywards. Their reasoning is that the flapping of the captive bird will attract other pigeons to the area, allowing the hunters to take pot-shots at them. A few birds may be shot, later to be made into a delicious salmi which is a speciality of the area, but whether this rather complicated method of hunting wood pigeons is the most effective one or not is debatable. However, everyone has a good time, with the possible exception of the decoy pigeon, and it certainly does wonders for the armagnac trade.

I am not a hunter but have no fixed viewpoint on the subject. However, the presence of hunting does allow me to see wild deer frequently roaming through the woods and the countryside. This is a pleasure that I would not have if there were no hunting; deer being extremely destructive, the farmers would have annihilated them long ago if it were not for the hunting lobby. There are also major differences between hunting as carried out in a French village compared to hunting in Britain. There is no class connotation to hunting in France – it is an activity shared by all social classes. Most importantly, the animals hunted by the *paysan*s are not just killed for sport but find their way to the table, where they are much enjoyed. In fact they are probably killed in a reasonably humane way, in that they are taken by surprise and shot and do not have to suffer either the journey to the slaughterhouse or any of its associated horrors. I often wonder at the mentality of those people who oppose the hunt but buy their poultry and eggs from a supermarket.

The church played an important part in the village life and was usually full on Sundays. After the service many of the congregation would retire to the adjacent *auberge*, there to partake of their Sunday lunch *en famille*. Life in Duhort could still be regulated by the church bell. In one corner house of the square there lived alone an aged woman who, during the ten years we lived there, never to my knowledge left the village. Her only visible occupation was to cross the village square at regular hours during the day to pull on the rope of one of the two bells which adorned the church tower. One did not need a clock in Duhort. The only exception to this lady's weekday routine was when she would toll the two bells and let their mournful chimes announce the death of someone in the village. The sound of the death knell would bring awareness of mortality to one's ears, and with it not only a sense of loss that one of the villagers had died, but also a sense of belonging to a close community.

There is a timeless stillness in the small villages of France which is accentuated by the sound of church bells. Working or relaxing in the garden under the summer sun, I would become conscious of an almost palpable feeling of continuity and timelessness and feel at peace with the world.

9

DUHORT – 2

One hot summer afternoon after a couple of hours of gardening I crossed the road to have a chat and a glass of wine with Robert. Opening the gate and strolling into the yard, I saw him sitting quietly outside the forge upon the upturned empty oil barrel which was his favourite seat. His eyes were closed and he held in one hand an empty glass and in the other the end of a piece of string. On the other side of the yard an old barn door was balanced on its edge at about 45 degrees from the vertical and supported in that position by a large stick wedged between the door and the ground. The other end of the piece of string was tied to the stick.

'What are you doing?' I asked him.

'Trapping pigeons,' he replied.

Looking closer at the ground beneath the door, I could see that it was covered fairly liberally with corn.

'The pigeons come for the corn and while they are busy pecking away I pull the string. The door falls and *bim bam boum*! there you are,' he explained.

'How many *bim bam boums* have you had so far?' I asked him.

'None as yet,' he replied. 'The pigeons seem reluctant to come.'

'If I was a pigeon, I would keep as far away as possible from that bloody contraption,' I told him. 'A French pigeon has to have been born with enough sense to steer clear of it and any associated *bim bam boums*!'

With a shrug of his shoulders Bikini muttered, 'Peut-être.' He rose slowly from his oil barrel, scratched the back of his neck and then together we went into the cool gloom of the forge to quench our thirst.

Later, I wondered what exactly Bikini intended to do with any pigeon that had been foolish enough to wander in range of his lethal door. Did he intend to eat it? I could not imagine how he could have prepared for the table a pigeon flattened by a door weighing well over 50 pounds and falling subject to Newton's laws of motion. Some sort of sandwich, perhaps, or maybe pigeon pâté.

Somebody once said, unkindly, that the French will eat anything that flies, swims, walks, crawls or slithers across God's earth. While this is not at all true, there are a number of creatures which are devoured here with relish which would, for one reason or another, be repugnant to the majority of Anglo-Saxons. I have developed a liking for frogs' legs, particularly in a *sauce provençale*. Snails I can take or leave alone, mainly because I find that the garlic sauce in which they are served merits something better than the fairly tasteless piece of often rather rubbery flesh which lies at the bottom of the shell. I draw the line, however, at ortolans, or buntings, as they are also called. These are very tiny birds indeed and they are regarded as a great delicacy in the Landes, where although they cannot be purchased commercially, their sale being illegal, there is really nothing to stop them being privately bred for the table.

My encounter with ortolans occurred one New Year's Eve, when we had been invited by our neighbours to dine and celebrate the New Year with them. Marie Christine, an excellent cook, and her husband Jean Pierre, who enjoys his wife's cooking, are a Landaise couple well versed in local tradition, and especially so when it comes to food and wine. Knowing the high standard of Marie Christine's skill in the kitchen, we were both looking forward to an excellent dinner, which she had promised would include a surprise dish.

The surprise when it came was one that I could have happily missed out on. After we had enjoyed our first bottle of champagne Marie Christine, with a certain air of reverence, brought a dish to the table. It held a dozen tiny naked birds, evidently cooked in a fragrant sauce, each bird being no larger than a man's thumb. Marie Christine then handed each one of us a towel and explained to Annie and me the correct way to eat ortolans. To begin with, one places the towel over one's head in the same manner as if one was inhaling a nasal decongestion vapour. Then between finger and thumb one picks up the bird by its head and, holding the head, places the rest of the bird in the mouth. One then bites through the neck before replacing the decapitated head on the dish. The entire bird, less its head, is then slowly chewed. The purpose of the towel is to ensure that none of the aroma is lost in transit between the dish and the mouth.

Jean Pierre was evidently proud that his wife was serving such a rare and traditional dish and both he and his wife disappeared under their towels. Annie, looking at me with some trepidation, did the same. Looking around the table at the three veiled heads now bowed over their plates, I had the feeling that I was indulging in some sort of traditional North African ceremony, and looking at the tiny naked corpses laid out on the dish, I realised that this was the point where my innate British culture finally overcame my adopted French one.

'Jean Pierre,' I enquired. 'The birds have not been cleaned?'

'Of course not,' he replied, emerging momentarily from beneath his towel. 'They are far too small for that. However, they have been fed only on cereal for the past few weeks and so they are perfectly all right.'

That was the last straw. I felt like a visitor to Arabia being offered a lamb's eyeball at a banquet given in his honour. I looked at the diminutive creatures again. Not only was I expected to crunch on their tiny bones, I was also expected to chew on their intestines. It was a difficult moment. The last thing I wished to do was to offend our hosts, but I just could not eat the birds in that fashion.

'Marie Christine,' I asked. 'Would you mind if I used a knife and fork?'

Three incredulous French heads appeared from beneath

their towels to watch me delicately trying to carve an inch-long bird with a table knife.

'Delicious,' I exclaimed, nibbling at a quarter-inch long drumstick.

Three sets of French eyebrows were raised and then three sets of French shoulders were shrugged before the three French heads disappeared once more under their towels to begin crunching.

That was the first and last time I have attempted to eat ortolans.

These minute birds apart, the south-west may not be the only region of France renowned for its gastronomy but it certainly does have a rich and varied cusine that would satisfy the most demanding epicure. It is of course famous for the production of foie gras. The preparation of this highly priced delicacy is usually undertaken by the farmer's wife, who will feed or *gave* the duck or goose and later prepare the liver for the table. Other local specialities centre mainly on dishes of duck, goose and chicken, with *confit de canard* probably the most popular. The fishing ports of Cap Breton and St Jean de Luz provide a plethora of fish from anchovies to tuna, as well as a wide variety of shellfish and from Arcachon come quantities of delicious oysters. The warm soil and the temperate climate allow the cultivation of most fruit and vegetables, while the heavily forested areas are rich with a wide variety of mushrooms, of which the much sought after *cèpe* is undoubtably the king. Add to this abundance of fresh local produce the wines of Bordeaux and Jurançon as well as many other smaller vineyards, and one can understand why the south-west is a gourmet's paradise. The crowning glory to this list of delights is the flow of armagnac from the traditional distilleries of the Landes and the Gers.

Jour de Fête – 1

The French, and to my knowledge the Spanish, are still capable of enjoying themselves in a late night crowd without the event degenerating into a free-for-all and eventually requiring police intervention. Along with probably most other villages in the south-west, Duhort has two fixed fêtes each year, one during the spring and the other much later on in early September. The first visible signs that a fête is approaching is when Damien, the village *cantonnier* – the person employed by the community to keep the village tidy – begins to hang coloured lights and bunting between the trees that surround the village square. This activity, in which Damien, precariously balanced upon the village ladder, has the benefit of advice from various onlookers as to the correct height and angle of the decorations, continues for about a week or so, and then the first caravans appear and stalls and carousels are erected. Meanwhile, at the local *auberge* a 15-metre long bar is erected under the arcades. Finally the loud bang from a single firework on a Friday at midday is the signal that the fête is officially open. The first visitors to appear are always the local children, who after enjoying a ride upon the roundabouts scamper around the rest of the attractions, poking their inquisitive noses into the mysteries and delights of the candy and other stalls. However, apart from this activity, the afternoon passes relatively quietly. During the evening the square becomes filled with young men and their girlfriends from nearby villages, who alternate between the shooting galleries and the bar. Eventually when their shooting becomes too erratic, they engage in simulating violent accidents on the electric bumper cars, which are, happily, constructed for such purposes. Tiring of this, they then join the disco in the village hall. The highlight of the fête is Saturday, when in the evening there is a procession of floats which have been carefully prepared by the villagers over the preceding months. Although the floats are of an amazingly high standard for a tiny village, the most popular part of the parade is always the appearance of the 'Duhort Majoreux'. These are some 20 or so agricultural workers dressed in drag. They are all fairly hefty individuals and, dressed in pink tutus and rose-pink blouses with heavy make-up, they make an hilarious caricature of a parade of majorettes. Their leader, all of 18 stone, signals changes to

115

their fairly complicated marching and dancing routine by shrill blasts upon a whistle, while their musical accompaniment is provided by a battery-operated record player carried in an old pram behind the troupe. Arriving at each corner of the village square, the Majoreux break from their marching and in response to energetic whistle-blowing from the leader complete a series of formation dancing. Before starting the parade the men concerned are always a little self-conscious about their feminine attire, and it requires a certain amount of *floc* to be drunk by each member before they have the collective courage to start their performance. However, the consumption of this nerve-steadying drink does nothing to detract from their skill in performing but, rather beneficially, lends a certain air of abandon to their dance routine. The Duhort Majoreux are in great demand at all the local village fêtes, often travelling as far as 50 miles away to participate in a carnival.

Towards eight o clock, the evening meal is held under a marquee, with venison provided by the local hunt the star item on the menu. Annie and I were always amused by the way that a sudden silence would fall upon the village, a silence only broken by the clash of knives and forks as the villagers attacked the serious business of eating. Once replete with food and wine, most of the people head back to the square for dancing. On the Saturday night the dancing commences in a traditional style with couples circulating between the stalls to the sound of accordion music. Later still, at some time after midnight, the dancing moves to the village hall and rock music is provided for the teenagers. Sunday, the last full day of the fête, sees a lunchtime repeat of the parade of floats and an afternoon of spectacular *Course Landaise* in the arena. That night, the entertainment commences with a firework display on the lake of the local mill and finishes with a disco that continues well into the early hours of Monday morning. During the whole period of the fête the bar at Les Arcades is always open and does a roaring trade serving prodigious quantities of wine and beer.

Living, as we did, fronting the square, we had little if any sleep during these three nights. It was, however, enjoyable to see traditional dancing in the village square and generally to soak up and be part of the atmosphere of the fête. I found it remarkable that such a small village could furnish so much entertainment. Perhaps as many as 400 or 500 people thronged the square at night. Copious amounts of alcohol in one form or another were consumed and yet there was never an outbreak of trouble serious enough to require the forces of law and order. Perhaps during the last hours of the disco a couple of youths who had over-imbibed would exchange a punch or two, but it stopped at that. Frequently we would leave our car parked outside our front door during the whole of the fête, but it was never in any way damaged.

Village fêtes apart, there were other times when Duhort or other nearby villages burst into life of an evening. A small travelling circus would appear for a week, installing itself on the square, or an orchestra would give a concert of dance music. On these latter occasions a temporary bandstand and seating would be erected. Some families, however, would prefer to occupy the tables and chairs on the terrace of the local café and enjoy their evening to the strains of *Tea for Two* and other classics of a different time.

A marriage in the village church is another occasion for festivity. The population of Duhort has as its nucleus no more than some half-dozen or so families, and the same is probably true for most of the country villages of France. Over time, these families have become enlarged through marriage and as a consequence these days one finds that virtually everyone in the village is related to each other in one way or another. A village marriage is the occasion for a family get-together and so it is normal to find anywhere between 200 and 300 guests attending such a wedding. It is usually a three-day event, organised to take care of all the age groups, with a dance for the older people, a disco for the younger generations and regular feasts, all sandwiched between a Friday and early the following Monday morning. The ceremony itself takes place on the Saturday, first in the *mairie*, where Monsieur le Maire performs the obligatory civil marriage, after which the bride

117

and groom, followed by close relations, usually proceed across the square to the church for the optional religious ceremony. Later come the photographs, which at Duhort are frequently taken in the village square, and the hundreds of guests, once seated upon the specially erected stand, are chivvied into poses for the wedding album. This episode completed, it is back to the village hall, because by now it is time for an aperitif. Everywhere in France arrivals and departures from a wedding are the opportunity for car drivers to make as much noise as possible, and the loud blaring of klaxons has unharmoniously superceded the need for the church bell in announcing that a wedding is taking place.

'I have a wife and so forth'
William Congreve: *The Way of the World*

My passion for this simple life in the French countryside was not shared to the same extent by Annie. It was not that she wished to return to Paris or to live in any large city, but she did feel that village life was fairly constrained. She had begun an interest in the theatre and belonged to an amateur dramatic school in Mont-de-Marsen, which she attended a couple of evenings a week. Mont-de-Marsen is some 20 miles from Duhort and Annie did not appreciate too much the drive home through the lonely countryside, often very late at night. Apart from Mont-de-Marsen our nearest city was Pau, which, although a beautiful city looking on to the Pyrenees and possessing extensive shopping facilities, lies some 35 miles away from Duhort and could hardly be called convenient. Briefly, Annie complained about the lack of daily activity, the sight of Bikini leading a couple of his brother's cows across the square being insufficient to satisfy her Parisian need for excitement. I did understand her feelings and so rather reluctantly agreed that we move house, but only after insisting that although I was prepared to move nearer to a town I was not willing to live in one. Annie's desire was to move nearer to the coast and even further south into that part of France known as the 'Pays Basque'.

Finally we agreed to put the house on the market and Annie made many trips to the area around Bayonne, some 90 miles away from Duhort. Here she contacted a number of estate agents and spent time viewing numerous houses. In the autumn of 1997 we sold our house in Duhort and purchased another in Ustaritz, a large village a little to the south of Bayonne. We were still in the countryside, albeit not the remote countryside of the Landes, but we were within easy reach of the coastal resorts of Biarritz and St Jean de Luz. Annie was happy.

10

'CONFUSION NOW HATH MADE HIS MASTERPIECE'
Shakespeare: *Macbeth*

The related sale and purchase of the houses, however, did not pass too smoothly and again I found myself in a situation bordering upon the incomprehensible for an Anglo-Saxon. But I had lived long enough in France to know that everything would be all right on the night and that whatever the complications, the French *Système D* would find a way around them. The complication went this way: When purchasing a house in France it is the custom that as soon as the selling price is agreed the buyer pays a deposit of between 5 per cent and 10 per cent of the purchase value and at the same time agrees the date for completion of the contract and subsequent occupation of the premises. Once this deposit has been paid, the buyer is committed to either buying the house at the completion date or losing this deposit to the benefit of the seller. The deposit cheque is made out to the seller but is withheld by either the estate agent or the solicitor until the final completion of the contract. On the other hand, the seller is now obliged to sell the house at the agreed price to the buyer or to refund the deposit, along with an equal amount of financial compensation, because he has broken the commitment. The idea behind this procedure is good in that it protects the buyer from gazumping and also reassures the seller that his house is really sold. The only let-out clause in the agreement is the buyer's inability to negotiate a loan, should he require one for the purchase.

120

The sale of our house presented no particular problem, it was in the purchase of the house in Ustaritz that the problems began. We had bought a house left empty by the death of an elderly, childless widow who had named her nephews as the inheritors. Given that there were no direct descendants and no parents alive, she was entitled under French law to do this. The house was put up for sale by the widow's brother, who travelled down from Paris to meet us at the estate agent's office and agree the selling price and the date when we would take posession of the property. Once this had been agreed, we signed the necessary documents which committed us to buy the house and everybody shook everyone else's hand. The estate agent then smilingly requested my cheque for an amount equal to 10 per cent of the value of the house and I duly took out my chequebook and signed away the amount requested. I must add that I was assured that the cheque would not be cashed until such time as the final contract was signed on the completion date, unless of course I opted out of the deal, in which case I would lose my deposit. So far so good. We had agreed a date at the end of August for vacating our house in Duhort to our buyer and a date a day later for occupying the house in Ustaritz. Everything seemed to be going smoothly and we returned home to Duhort to spend the next few weeks preparing for our removal – and to see a great deal of our buyers, who would come and go with a tape measure, pencil and graph paper to decide whereabouts exactly they would place the antique table they had inherited from Aunt Mathilde and other such pressing matters.

Then, just when everything seemed to be progressing well, came the thunderbolt. Telephoning the estate agent one day to tell him that we would like to visit our new house to decide on the renovations that we thought were necessary, he calmly informed me of a slight problem. I should have known, of course, that somewhere along the line there would have to be a problem. The widow's brother had, it seemed, no legal right to put the house on the market as it had been left to her nephews. The nephews had to agree the sale, but unfortunately as they were not yet 18 years of age they could not give their consent without the matter passing through the hands of a solicitor who would be appointed to guard the children's interest. Furthermore, as it was now late in July virtually the whole of France was *en vacances* and no solicitor was available. This information was passed to me in a very apologetic manner, rather in the tone of a nervous second officer informing the captain of the *Titanic* that the wretched ship had sprung a leak. Annie and I were now in the position of having to move out of our house in a few weeks' time and camp on the street, or to cancel our own sale, handsomely compensating our buyer. While it was possible in this case to cancel our purchase and retrieve our deposit, we were unlikely to receive any compensation as the house had been put up for sale illegally because the nephews had not given their agreement. We were in a situation that in my engineering days we would have referred to as being SNAFU.

A call for help to my own solicitor elicited the helpful reply of: 'What do you want me to do?' and my reply that the reason for my call was to ask him what I should do was met with a heavy silence. I turned once more to the estate agent, who assured me that everything could be arranged between people of good will and that things would sort themselves out in the end. Eventually *Système D* came to the rescue and it was agreed that we could move into the house on a sort of squatter basis, but on the condition that we were not to make the slightest alteration to any part of the house until the sale was finally completed, as everyone except me was sure that the nephews would agree to the sale. There was, of course, no objection to my tidying up the garden, which was knee-deep in weeds.

A couple of days before our removal date we signed the final contract with our buyer in front of our solicitor. There was one happy moment for me when our buyer handed over his cheque for the purchase of our house, but it was a short-lived one. It was made out to our solicitor, who turned to me with a gracious smile and said, 'I'll take care of that until we can complete the purchase of your house in Ustaritz.' He put the cheque in his desk drawer, which was then closed with a click of finality. 'Incidentally,' he added, 'we will not be able to do anything for the next two weeks in any case as I'm off on holiday.'

We moved to Ustaritz as planned and remained as squatters for a month. There were times when I awakened at night sweating from dreams where I saw our solicitor with my cheque and a pneumatic blonde on the beach in Copacabana, but in the end everything turned out well. Annie's reaction to the constraint that we must not change the house in any way was typically French. She called in the builders to knock down a dividing wall between the kitchen and the dining room the day after we moved in.

'Et in Arcadia ego'
Anon

The Pays Basque, or the country of the Basques, covers a total area of some 20,000 square kilometres, of which only 3,000 square kilometres are in Aquitaine, while the remainder lies across the frontier in Spain. The country stretches from Bayonne in the north across the Pyrenees into Spain and Navarre in the south. Westward the Basque country begins west of Bilbao in Spain and reaches eastwards towards St Christau and the river Aspe in France. The origins of its people and of their language remain a mystery and it has even been suggested that the Basques are indeed the descendants of the original prehistoric cave dwellers who have left their wall paintings amongst the caves of the Pyrenees. Whatever. Details of their early history are sparse but it is probable that during the sixth century the Basques, pushed by the Visigoths from their settlements in the valley of the Spanish river Ebro, founded the Kingdom of Vasconie in the Pyrenees. It is even possible that many of those Basques who crossed the Pyrenees mingled with the people of Aquitaine, eventually to become the Gascons, but that those who remained in the mountain area clung ferociously to their language and traditions. The Basque language, L'euskara, which is basically common to

123

both the French and the Spanish Basques, while having absorbed certain Roman words bears no relationship to any other known language.

The beauty of the Basque country lies in its proximity to the Pyrenees and to the surfable beaches of the Atlantic coast. The pure air and the green undulating countryside dotted with tiny picturesque villages, while giving it the air of a rediscovered Eden, also places it high on the list of French tourist resorts, consequently making it subject to an annual summer invasion. Certainly there are advantages to life in a tourist zone, not the least of which is the pleasure of living in a beautiful area; but more than that, we benefit throughout the year from all those attractions, be they museums, art galleries, restaurants, sporting facilities and so on, which have been developed with the tourist in mind.

The obverse side of the coin is the saturation of all these facilities as well as the crammed road and public transport systems, the latter frequently degenerating into complete chaos in France due to well-timed air and rail strikes during the months of July and August. These are the months when it behoves local residents to remain in their gardens alongside their barbecues and swimming pools, if they are fortunate enough to have them, or else to take their own holiday in half-empty Paris, travelling in the opposite direction to the hordes of Parisians, Belgians, Dutch, Germans and British who are clogging the highways between Paris and Biarritz. Amongst these happy holidaymakers the Dutch are perhaps the most noticeable on the roads. They have caravans. While it is true that many visitors of all nationalities are equipped with caravans, the Dutch are peculiar in that apparently they all have one. In fact the profusion of Dutch car-caravan combinations in any specific summer gridlock is such that I have often wondered whether the purchase of a car in Holland does not automatically qualify the purchaser for a free caravan.

However, from the month of September through to June the Basque country can be enjoyed at leisure, especially as the climate is such that the weather is often at its best from September to November. It may be true that Biarritz enjoys approximately the same rainfall as Manchester and that the south-west in general has earned itself the sobriquet of 'the chamberpot of France', but most of the rain tends to fall in the spring and early summer, while for the rest of the year the sun shines more often than not. Again, in the early part of the year Biarritz is frequently the warmest place in France and we have often enjoyed a lunch of fresh seafood sitting on the sunny terrace of our favourite restaurant at St Jean de Luz with a January temperature of 70°F.

'The terrorist and the policeman both come from the same basket'
Joseph Conrad: *The Secret Agent*

The Spanish Pays Basque has for many years sought its independence from Spain and that country has been and still is the seat of violent terrorist activity carried out by ETA, the Basque independence terrorist organisation. The French Basque, although fiercely defending his language and culture, has not stooped to the same level. A French Basque is more likely to proudly proclaim that he is firstly a Basque but will then add that he is secondly a French citizen by choice. Given this insularity, Annie and I had some reservations as to our ability to integrate into a Basque environment but up to now our doubts have proved unfounded. We have both found the local people to be friendly and, in fact, perhaps as a result of the tourist trade, even more welcoming to strangers than the Gascons of the Landes.

Ustaritz, situated 6 miles south of Bayonne, is the ancient capital of Labourd, one of the three French Basque provinces, and as can be expected there is a very strong influence of Basque culture in the village, an influence almost strong enough to give rise to a feeling that we are really not living in a part of metropolitan France but in some French overseas dominion. There is also a strong feeling of Basque nationalism, and since we have lived here there has, at least on one occasion, been a distant bang in the middle of the night as

125

someone has explosively emphasised his own feeling of independence. However, such expressions of violence are
extremely rare and take place during the still, quiet hours of
the early morning with no resultant risk to life or limb, except
perhaps to the perpetrator. Buildings seem to be the target,
and as the site chosen is usually the local tax office, even
though one may be fundamentally opposed to violence and
the wanton destruction of property, there could be worse
targets for the venting of spleen. The only other manifestation
of independent Basque feeling can be seen expressed by
occasional bands of graffiti adorning some of the village walls.
These graffiti are invariably written in the Basque language
and consequently indecipherable to the majority of passers-by,
and so seem to me to be a waste of time and effort on the part
of the person yielding the paint spray. A sort of preaching to
the converted, as it were.

Life generally in Ustaritz is very pleasant and to be recom-
mended, and so while, unlike Annie, I do miss the complete
stillness and peace of the unspoilt Landes, I find that life in
Ustaritz has its own charm. The only constraint that we have
found so far is that upon giving the house a badly needed coat
of paint we were obliged to keep it in the traditional colours
of white for the walls and either Basque red or Basque green
for the woodwork. We can live with that.

Jour de Fête – 2

The Basques are extremely fond of fêtes and there are numerous times during the year when the villages becomes alive with
one. Bars spring up along the streets in the centre of a village
and there are parades and dancing to traditional, if not har-
monious, Basque music. Above all, the Basques enjoy watching and participating in feats of strength and during certain
fêtes the men of the village will demonstrate their prowess by
lifting and carrying 500-pound weights and other heavy and
unlikely objects, to the appreciative applause of the onlookers.

126

How half the male population has escaped being ruptured is somewhat of a mystery to me.

Ustaritz is close to the city of Bayonne and it is perhaps for this reason that fête days in the village do not have the same innocence as those we experienced in the Landes. The five-day July fête in Ustaritz rapidly degenerates into a contest to decide who can consume the most alcohol in the shortest possible time. Late in the evenings and during the nights the village bars become crowded and rowdy; but while violence flares occasionally, such outbursts remain at the fist-fight level and there is little vandalism. It is the propriety of the streets in the centre of the village which suffers the most from being exposed to five nights of drunken revelry.

The Basque, drunken or not, can, however, be trusted to pay for his drinks at these times, or so I am assured by the local bar owners. A considerable amount of money is spent on various forms of alcohol over the fête days, enough in fact to ensure the winter profitability of all the village bars, but even at the height of a night's festivity, with complete confusion reigning at the bar counter and numerous rounds of a dozen or more drinks being ordered at the same time, there is very little chance that they will not be paid for. It appears that the Basque is honest.

La Petite Auberge – 1

No mention of the village of Ustaritz would be complete without a reference to La Petite Auberge, a small hotel, café, restaurant, bar and tobacconist in the old centre of the village. It differs from every other similar establishment that I have come across in France in that the bar is comfortable. Whereas in Britain the pub is a social centre where people gather to pass a friendly evening in warmth and comfort, the French bar is usually austere and reflects the nation's culture that social activities are either home or restaurant based. In France, people tend to visit a bar during the day or early evening whenever they feel the need for a quick refreshment. They

127

will stand at the bar, have their drink, then leave, preferring to reserve any bar-based social contact for the summer months, when they will happily spend part of an hour or so on a Saturday afternoon, or on a weekday in the early evening before dinner, sitting on a café terrace enjoying the sun. In the majority of French cafés the bar itself is usually stark, and the best one can hope for in terms of furniture is a few small wooden tables and some hard-backed chairs. Entertainment is usually offered by a couple of noisy pin-tables and that equally noisy table football game, Babyfoot.

La Petite Auberge is a family-run affair and *la patronne*, known as Maddo, which is one form of the French diminutive for Madelaine, had the bright idea of equipping the bar with cushioned armchairs and settees. The result of this furnishing, combined with the antiquity of the building and the hospitality of the family, produce an atmosphere very close to that of a typical British country pub. Regular customers, and in the season tourists, can make themselves comfortable in the bar, where there is always plenty of conversation. There are no pin or Babyfoot tables, but Maddo and her son Hervé are always ready to engage a customer in a friendly contest of Yams, this being an entertaining if fairly simple game played with dice. Maddo is also an excellent cook and is renowned in the area for her *poule farcie*, and of course for those standard south-west dishes: *magret* and *confit de canard*. Hervé's wife Monique contributes a *tarte aux poires* to the dessert menu, and the final result of their combined skills makes La Petite Auberge one of the best reasonably priced restaurants in the area.

La Petite Auberge – 2

I was propping up the corner of the bar, letting the cool brew of an excellent Abbaye Leffe slake my summer thirst, and Maddo was attending to the wants of another customer before setting up the dice for our usual game of Yams, when Hervé made an appearance through the restaurant doorway. He was accompanied by his motorcycle, which is normally garaged between tables 5 and 6: in which position it does add a further point of interest to the restaurant decor although conflicting somewhat with the ancient tapestries that adorn the walls.

Hervé striding into the bar, clothed in black and with his head beneath an all-encompassing crash helmet, is an awe-inspiring sight, putting one in mind of *The Thing from Outer Space*. However, removing the helmet reveals a smiling face and one is immediately put at ease. After his usual greeting and handshake, he told me that he had just returned from a quick shopping expedition at the nearest Spanish supermarket, a commercial enterprise mainly aimed at the French purchaser and only some 20 minutes away by road for a normal driver, although probably nearer to 10 for Hervé on his souped-up chariot. He was happy to list for me all the items he had bought and to tell me how much cheaper they were in Spain than France.

'I have three bottles of sherry, a carton of cigarettes, and a few cans of olives for less than three hundred francs,' he said.

'What would that be in euros?' I asked.

This remark brought Maddo as well as a couple of other regulars into the conversation.

'Given,' said Maddo, 'that a great number of people who come into this bar still reckon their money in old francs, which was a currency replaced by the new franc nearly forty years ago, it will be some time before anybody here can understand the cost of anything marked up in euros. It will be a disaster, if you ask me.'

'Well, sometimes I still think in old francs,' said Martine, the wife of Jean Pierre, a stalwart regular at the bar. 'Although the conversion to new francs is easy – you just divide the amount in old francs by a hundred. Maybe it's just a case of nostalgia.'

'The funny thing is that some young people who were not even born at the time of the change still talk in old francs,' added Jean Pierre.

'I have to admit that it does seem peculiar that the French still cling to the old franc,' I said. 'Even some newspapers still report large sums such as Lottery winnings in both old and new francs. It was not like that in the UK when they brought in decimalisation, and that was not an easy calculation, having to divide the old money by two point four to make the conversion from old pence into new.'

I was working over in Northern Ireland at the time of the UK decimalisation, and spending one Saturday afternoon in Blackrock, a small seaside village, when rain, which is never far away in Ireland, suddenly descended in a drenching shower and I popped into a nearby 'penny bazaar' for shelter. It was a typical 1930s establishment with long counters displaying a host of cheap souvenirs, while its Irishness manifested itself in a framed portrait of President John Kennedy, complete with a halo illuminating his forehead, priced at two shillings and sixpence. The proprietor, a diminutive, voluble Irishman, was at his wits' end with the problems of converting the marked-up prices on his myriad souvenirs into decimal coinage.

'Will you tell me,' he asked, shoving a new 2p coin under my eyes, 'what this is worth?'

'Look,' I replied, 'you have to multiply it by two point four to convert it back, which means that in old money it would be nearly five pence.'

Like most engineers of that time, I always carried a slide rule in my breast pocket and taking it out, I offered to spend some time with him converting his prices into decimal coinage.

The Irishman looked at the slide rule aghast.

'Jasus!' he exclaimed. 'Don't tell me that I have to learn to use one of them things.'

'No, of course not,' I assured him. 'It's just a bit quicker for multiplying or dividing, that's all, and all you have to do is divide all your old prices by two point four to arrive at the price in new money. I don't mind helping you for half an hour or so and it won't take as long as you think it will.'

'Well, I shan't be bothering,' said the proprietor. 'Because in my opinion this new money thing will not catch on at all.'

Some days later I was in a village pub deep in the Cotswolds and proffered a new 10p piece to pay for my glass of cider. The barmaid looked at it dubiously.

130

'I'm not sure that we are taking those yet,' she informed me.

Those two episodes apart, so far as I can remember in my experience, the conversion to decimalisation passed fairly quickly and fairly painlessly in the UK. Indications are that it will not be the same when France takes to the euro in 2002.

11

'HOW CAN YOU GOVERN A COUNTRY WHICH HAS 246 VARIETIES OF CHEESE?'

Ernest Mignon: *Les Mors du Général*

French politics are not devoid of complication. The French people elect their President to serve a seven-year term, and once they are elected there is no constitutional way of dismissing them from office. The President's first job is to nominate a Prime Minister, who then forms a government. So far so good. However, parliamentary (legislative) elections are held every five years, although the President may call one at any time during their mandate. Complications first arose when, after voting into power the socialist François Mitterrand as President in 1981, the electorate voted for a right-wing majority at the 1986 legislative elections. The result was a socialist President with a right-wing Parliament.

The French called this situation 'co-habitation', and many seemed almost in favour of it, possibly believing that the conflict of ideals between the head of state and the head of government would produce some sort of balance in government policy. However, between 1986 and 1988, Mitterrand and his right-wing Prime Minister Jacques Chirac created a strained atmosphere which was evident to everyone in France. In 1993, after another right-wing legislative victory, Mitterrand chose Edouard Balladur as his Prime Minister. Edouard, very much the gentleman, was to demonstrate that he was adept at the 'softly softly' approach, and at least so far as the public were concerned the relations between the President and the Prime Minister remained amicable for the remainder of Mitterrand's term.

Whatever his other strengths or weaknesses, François Mitterrand was nothing if not a survivor. Initially he had survived and worked under the Vichy regime and then later became involved with the Resistance. After the liberation of France he worked with the government of General De Gaulle before finally turning to socialism. In 1981 he was elected President, and after fulfilling his seven-year term was re-elected for a further term in 1988. A varied career but, like the renowned Vicar of Bray, he could be described as one who was able to survive the slings and arrows of outrageous political fortune. However, by the 1995 presidential elections the French were tired of any trace of socialism at any level of government and Jacques Chirac was elected President. He nominated Alain Juppé as Prime Minister, finally giving France a coherent right-wing government. Two years later the French were tired of Monsieur Juppé's policies, which were aimed at accelerating France into the cold, cruel, highly competitive and much vaunted global economy, and so they reverted to socialism at the 1997 legislative elections. The result was a right-wing President with a left-wing government, the mirror image of the Mitterrand–Balladur scenario.

Politics obviously does not escape from the general complication that pervades most aspects of French life. There are two major moderate right-wing parties: the Rassemblement pour le république (RPR) and the Union pour la démocratie française (UDF). The major left-wing party is the Socialists. The political division in France is now such that neither the right nor the left can obtain a majority without having recourse to the extreme political poles. The Socialists presently in power need to include both the Communists and the 'Green' parties in order to govern. The right wing, on the other hand, would obtain a majority if it was prepared to ally itself with the extreme right National Front, but given the stain left on the French conscience by the racial and other atrocities committed by Vichy, it could be political death for them if they were to make such an alliance.

I believe that all extreme points of view, whether they be political or religious or whatever, are targeted at the feeble-minded and that anyone who professes an extremist point of view is either attempting to manipulate the feeble-minded or are themselves suffering from feeble-mindedness. It is also possible that as none of the democratic political parties in France is capable of generating a majority in its own right but must rely upon an alliance with the political extremes of either communism or fascism to govern, then there may be a certain degree of feeble-mindedness associated with present-day French politics.

The beliefs that underpin French political thinking have their roots in the intellectual divisions which hearken back to the Revolution. Firstly, virtually all politicians are by definition intellectuals or technocrats, many of them having received their further education at the Ecole Nationale d'Administration. Consequently the socialists are intellectual socialists and are for the most part from middle-class backgrounds, perhaps seeing the inside of a factory for the first time as a visiting politician. They are not and probably have never been aware of the domestic and financial pressures which are the lot of the majority of people living a working-class life. In French socialism there have been very few, if any, of such characters as Ernest Bevin or Nye Bevan or Bessie Braddock or the host of other dedicated socialists who formed the first post-war Labour government in Britain and who at least understood from their own experiences the hardships associated with labouring for one's living. Neither are the right-wing politicians any better, for they are coloured by the same social and intellectual background, and when Monsieur Balladur in his role as Prime Minister travelled on the Paris metro to see how the majority of Parisians travel to work each day, it hit the television news. It was possibly the first time for many years that he had used such a form of transport.

The present socialist government in France is wrestling with the problem of how to maintain the liberal social security system, which requires high taxation to fund its deepening debts, while endeavouring to convince private enterprise, groaning under the present taxation level, to recruit more labour and diminish the high unemployment level, presently

134

hovering around 12 per cent of the workforce. So far they have come up with the brilliant idea of legally enforcing a 35-hour working week in the belief that if people work fewer hours then more people will be needed to complete any given task. The same logic could, of course, be applied to most civil engineering projects, where if mechanical shovels were to be replaced by men with spades then many job opportunities would be created. In fact, if the men were to be equipped with table-spoons instead of spades it would probably create enough jobs to absorb the entire unemployed population. With a government apparently locked into this sort of reasoning, it is not surprising that envious eyes are cast across the Channel and that in 1998 the British Prime Minister was regarded by many French politicians as having the ability to walk on water.

'Together for the sake of strife'
Charles Churchill: *The Rosciad*

In France, any action or proposed action which can be interpreted as a threat to the well-being of the pampered employees of any government-owned industry usually results in strike action. The strike is always timed to cause the maximum discomfort to the French citizen and to the rest of the world in general, and so with an almost monotonous regularity the French transport system usually grinds to a shuddering halt just in time to create havoc at the beginning and end of each holiday period.

If prizes were to be awarded to strikers on the basis of the frequency and the magnitude of the disruption caused by their action, then it is possible that Air France would win a gold medal. It often seems that Air France must be the only airline where the planes spend more time strikebound on the ground than they do in the air. Strangely enough, the remuneration offered to the pilots, and for that matter the rest of the Air France staff, compares more than favourably with other airlines and places them fairly high in the salary stakes. They appear, however, to have an almost childish glee in causing

135

chaos and consequently, although named as partners in the French 1998 World Cup football event and decorating their planes with images of dynamic footballers, they threatened to strike during the whole of the period. Any French resident familiar with travelling by Air France could have foretold this happening. The only hope for the harassed traveller is that eventually this airline will finally be privatised and have to compete on a level playing field with competitors, an event which when it happens will bring a sigh of relief to everybody who has been foolish enough to depend upon its service.

If state-owned Air France merits the gold, then the state-owned railway and metro service come in with a good silver. French railwaymen, a number of whom reach official railway retirement age when the majority of industrial managers are only halfway through their careers, specialise either in threatening to ruin or actually ruining Christmas for the majority of commercial traders and any others who rely upon rail transport over the festive season.

Finally, the bronze would have to go to the privately run road transport system, proving that it is not only the spoilt workers in nationalised industries that are possessed with the urge to create havoc. Lorry drivers do not score so highly in the frequency league table as Air France, who are unbeatable on that score, but their strikes have more punch. Lorry drivers just block all the roads and consequently bring all transport to a halt.

Transport workers apart, the need to demonstrate dissatisfaction publicly in the street often – but not always – combined with strike action, seem inherent in the French character. Recent manifestations of this have included secondary school pupils complaining of classroom conditions, and pensioners complaining about loss of purchasing power. Spice is added to this mix of social discontent by farmers dumping cabbages on airport runways and pig breeders turning their animals loose alongside government buildings.

The ability of the French people to live happy lives and to ignore the threat of transport paralysis which hangs, like some sword of Damocles, continually over their heads is just another proof of the capability of the human being to adapt to any set of circumstances. In the days that I worked in Northern Ireland I once took a train journey from Portadown to Belfast. Shortly after leaving Portadown, the train was subjected to violent and alarming blows on the sides of the carriages. None of the passengers, with the exception of myself, turned a hair or even looked up from their newspapers. We were passing through Lurgan, and I learned later that it was the habit of the local children there to throw rocks at the train and that apparently this was now considered to be quite a normal occurrence. Similarly every airline passenger now accepts the airport search of their personal belongings as routine, part of the procedure of air travel and not an infringement on their privacy.

However, not all is gloom, and if one can lose heart over the political scenario it has to be said that the wheels of French bureacracy seem to be turning more smoothly these days. I had recently to renew my residence permit, which expires every ten years, and presented myself at the nearest préfecture. The officials were polite and kindly, they furnished me with a list of the dozen or so items that I needed to prove that I was who I was and that I was still alive and still living in France, the photograph on my expired permit, my passport and my physical presence not being sufficient proof of this. Two weeks later, equipped with the required documentation, I visited the préfecture again and was once again met with courtesy. I signed the necessary application form, handed over all my documentation and was told I would receive my new residence permit sometime during the next three months. The whole procedure was, by French bureaucratic standards, handled quickly and efficiently and nobody even asked for my grandmother's maiden name.

'The customer is never wrong'
César Ritz

Spending the majority of my working life in the food industry, I became accustomed to the concept of customer service fairly early on in my career. It is a concept that was in its infancy in England when I left there in 1972 but has since made tremendous strides in the UK. In France it was unheard of in 1972 and remains more or less unheard of today.

The English had to overcome their negative approach to sales, and they have done so. On a holiday in the UK in the late 1970s I decided to buy a pair of shoes in a small Cotswold town, and seeing a pair that I liked in the window of a fairly large shop, I entered to buy them. Unfortunately, those on display were not in my size, and when I asked the salesgirl if she had the same shoes in a size eight she replied that they had none in stock. 'Size eight is a very popular size, you see,' she informed me.

'Is that why you don't have any in stock?' I asked. 'Because it is a very popular size?' The salesgirl looked at me with incomprehension in her eyes. When I then asked her about another pair in the window that had attracted my attention, she informed me that they were very expensive.

'That's all right,' I said. 'Could I try them on, please?'

'But they cost thirty pounds,' replied the shopgirl.

Even as late as the middle 1980s I found the same negative approach to selling in England. During a business trip to London, I called in one evening at a restaurant near Marble Arch for an evening meal, being tempted away for once from my usual Indian by the opportunity to sample fresh sea bass, my favourite fish. Once seated at the table, I ordered the sea bass and was immediately informed by the waiter that it was twenty pounds.

'That's a pretty large fish,' I replied. 'I don't think I could eat that amount, much as I love sea bass.'

'No, the cost is twenty pounds,' advised the waiter.

I had the impression in the England of the 1970s and early

138

1980s that the purchase of any item considered to be expensive by the salesman or saleswoman immediately classified the purchaser in their minds as some sort of extravagant wastrel who had absolutely no right to be throwing his money around in such a fashion. I felt resented, as if I belonged to a social class that should be put against a wall and shot. My more recent experiences in England, however, demonstrate that even in the far-flung north in such towns as Glossop the lessons of customer service have been well learned.

Unfortunately, the whole concept of customer service is foreign to the French mentality. Although many companies pay lip service to the idea, they do so without any clear understanding of what it means, and it is only the Anglo-Saxon and large French-owned multinationals in the main that endeavour to pass a customer service creed throughout their organisations. This phenomenon is not surprising; the French are not used to the competitiveness of privately owned business and the whole of French bureaucracy is based upon the idea that the entrepreneur is a bandit who will rob the state and exploit his workforce unless he is closely controlled and, anyway, goes the reasoning, he should not be working for himself but should be respectably employed as a civil servant or by a state-controlled industry.

How quickly the French can change this attitude is a debatable point, but change it they must if they are to compete in the world economy.

12

'AND MAKES ME END,
WHERE I BEGUN'

John Donne: '*A Valediction Forbidding Mourning*'

The love affair which I began with France some 50 years ago has continued through to the present day and I still love her, warts and all. She, in her turn, has been kind in granting me a wealth of experience, many happy memories, a fairly successful career, a loving spouse and a pleasant home. There is not much more that anyone can wish for in this world. While it is true to say that the years have changed both of us, the France of today still offers the same charms that captivated me as a student so many years ago and I love her because she has always offered me the way of life that meets all that I require to find happiness. I have learned to live with her bureaucracy and view its frustrations through French eyes. The Frenchman is born into a bureaucratic society and lives and dies within one, and as such becomes acclimatised to it. Throughout his life in all the many contacts he will be obliged to make with the administration, and even in many of the contacts that he will make in the commercial world, the first question he will be asked is: 'Do you have a dossier with us?' Finally when he dies the last bureaucratic act will be made by a representative of the civil authorities, who after verifying that the dead person is really the person that the surviving family claim him to be, will put the Republic's seal upon his coffin.

The Frenchman regards this bureaucracy in rather the same way as the Briton regards the weather. It exists, there is little that he can do about it and so although he will continually complain about it, for the most part he ignores it and gets on with enjoying his life.

I believe that I do at last understand the French mentality. Their desire for complete individual freedom and their rejection of all discipline, which sits uneasily with their dependence upon a benevolent father figure which today takes the form of the state. The Frenchman is like the spoilt son of a wealthy father. Determined to have his own way, he will act unheeding of the chaos he may cause to others and then run to Papa for help the moment things go wrong. Should Papa not be forthcoming with the required remedial action, then there will be tantrums. The Frenchman's tantrums are normally expressed in the form of a strike, but should the strike fail to obtain the results that he desires, then exactly like an overindulged child, he will bring the house down with his cries and his temper.

Basically insecure and with an almost paranoic belief that the world in general and the Anglo-Saxon world in particular, is plotting their individual downfall, the French consume more tranquillisers per head than the citizens of any other European country. Their first line of defence against the menacing world which they see outside the close circle of their own family and friends is to complain of the crassness of everybody else. The Frenchman is never devoid of a fresh story to tell of the many '*cons*' with whom apparently he meets each day. In his insecurity he loves nothing better than to engage in self-criticism, while really seeking approbation for his ideas and actions.

However, despite these rather negative aspects of their character, I like the French and admire their culture. They possess a tremendous energy, which they express daily in their enjoyment of life, and which can also be harnessed to attain greatness. They love spectacle and surprises but are also able to extract maximum enjoyment from the simplest of pleasures. They extend their *joie de vivre* to the workplace, where they are capable of great achievements. The word 'impossible', they will tell you, is not French. Socially they have the attributes of loyalty and generosity, and when one finally does get to know them they can become very faithful friends.

France has those social problems which are now fairly general in virtually all the cities of the western world. Juvenile crime, exaggerated by the use of drugs, is rampant and the newspapers seem to relish reporting the daily toll of murders, robbery and rape. In 1972 one could take the midnight metro to any station in Paris without the slightest feeling of insecurity, but this, unfortunately, is no longer true. Paris, however, differs from other large cities such as London in that the centre of the city is inhabited. Paris is never devoid of people in the streets and I still feel that I can walk through central Paris at 11 p.m. in reasonable security. I do not have the same feeling in London. Sometime in the late 1980s I was visiting there and staying at the Selfridges Hotel. I took my evening meal in a restaurant in Piccadilly and decided to walk back to the hotel along Regent Street and Oxford Street. It was only 10 p.m. but the pavements were deserted and I certainly did not feel myself to be in any security whatsoever. The main social problems in Paris are found in the outlying suburbs with high-rise apartment blocks and high immigrant populations with their associated racial problems. The centre of Paris is always alive with people.

The 'yob' culture which seems to have overtaken England has not yet arrived in France and I doubt that it will. There is an aggressiveness apparently innate in the Anglo-Saxon and the German that the Latin does not have. Perhaps this Anglo-Saxon aggressiveness enabled England to build and exploit an empire and perhaps it enabled Germany to produce mighty military regimes. The French also built an empire, and although they exploited it, they also regarded it as a 'mission to civilise', which is why perhaps for the most part the French ex-colonies still retain the vestiges of French culture. In any case, so far as the European Community is concerned, the days of military aggression and empire building are past history and Anglo-Saxon aggressiveness can now only find its outlet in such activities as football hooliganism and the violent actions of the animals rights supporters: to the distress of the majority of normal people. Despite their tendency towards bloody revolution, the French are not fundamentally aggressive. They do not look for trouble and only react violently when they suspect that their values or their way of life are under threat.

I love France because she has managed to gain and hold a leading industrial position in a technical age while still retaining an air of unchanging timelessness in the small towns and villages of the countryside. Despite the invasion of fast food, fast travel and fast communication, France still abounds with tiny villages, each with its homely *auberge* where *la patronne* welcomes the visitor with the cuisine she learned from her grandmother. The peasant still brings his produce to the market, offering for sale fresh produce and healthy corn-fed chickens which have ranged freely. The cheeses still taste of cheese and not of industrially produced soap. The bread is still freshly baked each morning and the wines are still incomparable. Perhaps this way of life is doomed. Perhaps Robert in Duhort tending his vines and ploughing his field with cattle is among the last generation that will live to this pattern, but I doubt it. Change comes slowly to deep France. The French *paysan* is not the the comic dim-witted bumpkin often portrayed in books and soap operas. On the contrary, he is not only educationally equal to his counterpart in any other society but culturally superior to most of them. He is so sure of his values and standards that although the tractor has long since replaced cattle as a motive force, it has been quietly absorbed into the daily work round and life in the villages continues much as it always has done.

Today many French people are probably consuming even more tranquillisers than usual as they wonder and worry as to how they are going to face up to the future and survive the pressures of savage industrial competition on a global scale. There is cause to worry. Highly paid for a 35-hour week. Five weeks of holiday per year, excluding a further ten days of religious or state holidays. Retirement at 60 with a generous pension. A more than generous Social Security system maintaining some 3 million unemployed and an ageing population. An excellent health service equipped with modern hospitals with no waiting lists and no shortage of beds. The list of benefits is long and costly and it is presently being paid for by swingeing taxation. This in its turn is crippling small businesses and acting as a brake upon their employment strategies. Like the mythical oozelum bird, which has one wing shorter than the other, the political system flies around in ever-decreasing circles until eventually it risks disappearing up its own backside. There is even a slight risk that the volatile French, faced with the apparent inability of any recent government to reassure them that their future is secure and their way of life unthreatened, may swing heavily towards the extreme right neo-fascist movement. They, like others of the same ilk before them, are all things to all men and their programme is simplicity itself: repatriate 3 million immigrants, thereby creating sufficient vacancies to absorb the unemployed, and then boost the economy by abolishing income tax. Happily, I believe that the French are too intelligent to swallow such a political line but in their frustration with their present ills they could just be inclined to try anything.

Longer-term, though, France is a naturally rich country and its people are hard-working, cultured and innovative. They have survived centuries of misrule, bloody revolutions, catastrophic wars and years of overpaid and inefficient bureaucracy. In reply they have fine-tuned their *Système D*, which is now heavily ingrained in their culture, and they have long since gained the habit of turning any of life's adversities to their own benefit in the end. Their way of life will continue to survive.

Finally, I love France because her countryside is full of variety and to travel from Strasbourg to Brittany or from Arras to Bayonne is to virtually enter another country. The scenery changes dramatically, the architecture changes completely, and the food and wine vary from region to region. Bordered by two oceans and possessed of two mountain ranges, France offers a wider range of lifestyle than perhaps anywhere else of a similar size on earth. Her climate ranges from that of the warm Mediterranean to the snows of the Alps, from the Continental climate of Alsace to the temperate climate of Brittany. However, no matter in which climate or in which area one finds oneself, be it in the industrial north or on the promenade of Nice, one is always aware that one is in France. France, through its culture, has achieved a remarkable unity amongst all its peoples, whether they be Normans, Bretons or Basques. They all share a common national identity. They are French. In the eighteenth century Britain strove to unite its people under the common identity of British. In this venture they failed to do as well as the French and today they are faced with devolution and perhaps even with independence for Scotland looming in the future and bringing the eventual break-up of the United Kingdom. Perhaps English culture was neither deep enough nor strong enough nor attractive enough to tempt either the Scots, Welsh or the Irish either to adopt it or to live alongside it.

In the meantime, here in the Basque country the sun is shining and the early June temperature is at a pleasant 28°C. Annie is sunbathing in the garden and the barbecue is waiting to be lit. The champagne is on ice and there is a good bottle of Bordeaux to be opened later, which should go down well with a slice of *brebis* (ewe's) cheese. Tomorrow we may go to the coast and swim in the surf or venture to explore a little more of the Pyrenees.

Whatever.

I think I'll stay here.